T. B Glanville

Abroad And at Home

T. B Glanville

Abroad And at Home

ISBN/EAN: 9783744734059

Printed in Europe, USA, Canada, Australia, Japan

Cover: Foto ©Thomas Meinert / pixelio.de

More available books at **www.hansebooks.com**

ABROAD AND AT HOME.

BY THE LATE

T. B. GLANVILLE,

CAPE GOVERNMENT EMIGRATION COMMISSIONER.

WITH PORTRAIT OF AUTHOR.

CAPE OF GOOD HOPE:

PORT ELIZABETH,   KIMBERLEY,
GODLONTON & CO.   B. D. GODLONTON & CO.

May be obtained of RICHARDS, SLATER & Co., GRAHAM'S TOWN, and of all Booksellers in chief Colonial Towns; and in LONDON of EDWARD STANFORD, 55, Charing Cross.

LONDON:
PRINTED BY WILLIAM CLOWES AND SONS,
STAMFORD STREET AND CHARING CROSS.

PREFACE.

In order to meet the wishes of my husband's numerous friends, I have gathered together some of his writings on various subjects not political. He resided nine years in India, and nineteen at the Cape, and these writings reach back to the time when he left the former country. Some have wished me to include the papers on the "Native Question" at the Cape; but it is not in my power to do so, as they were all written for the *Grahamstown Journal*, and I have no copies.

WILMOT GLANVILLE.

Topsham, Devon,
    Nov. 1878.

CONTENTS.

	PAGE
Gomuta Roya	1
The Guru's Dinner	17
What has England done for India?	23
The Indian Catastrophe	43
A Kaffir Sham-Fight	59
Reverence, and the want of it in this Colony	69
Looking-Glasses	103
Bell Voices	133
Two Old Books	151
An Amateur	163
Inside "The Bank"	177
Gladstone	189
Spurgeon	195
Dr. Parker	207
The Colonist at Home	225
At Looe with the Pilchards	239
South African Progress and Native Management	247

GOMUTA ROYA.

It is now some years ago, when a good friend of mine and myself, while on a tour in the Mysore, the land of Tippoo Sultan and Hyder Ali of rascally memory, thought it worth our while to go some twenty miles out of our road, to pay a visit to a famous giant statue, *Gomuta Roya* by name, belonging to the *Jaina Mallasthara*. And here let me say, that in doing so, we were following the example of no less a personage than the great Duke of Wellington, who, when Colonel Wellesley, rode over from Seringapatam, a distance of some seventy or eighty miles, to see this same colossus. Captain Basil Hall, too, made a *détour* from his line of route for the same purpose, and thought the statue of sufficient interest to give an account of it in his well-known work. In determining on this trip, therefore, we had all the pleasant feelings of pilgrims about to start upon a pathway beaten by no ignoble feet, to behold a shrine that had been gazed on by no vulgar curiosity.

Under the elevating influence of such thoughts we rolled up our rugs, just an hour before sunrise, took a cup of coffee and a biscuit, helped to pack up our traps, sent them off on the heads of coolies, despatched our cook, saddled our horses, and taking leave of our one-roomed hotel, quite wide open in front, which had been our reception-room, bedroom, dressing and dining-room for two or three days, we cantered out of Belloor before the good housewives of the town had chalked their door-steps.

A Hindoo town presents many a curious spectacle about the grey of the morning. In the hot summer months, especially, many of the respectable householders, wrapping themselves well up in their cloths, prefer to sleep through the night in the verandah to being baked in their little, low, no-windowed room. Accordingly, at break of day, there is a general unrolling of brown men all along the street. Here and there a well-shaved, shiny head appears released from the bundle, the mouth stretched to the eyebrows with the first yawn. Some half a dozen are sitting "up on end," looking at you with scarcely opened eyes, so sleepy and so vacant, that you are ready to pinch yourself by way of proof that you are not part and parcel of some night vision, and those the dreams. Others, again, are fairly on their legs, their long lithe limbs stretched out to the audible cracking of their joints; their drapery, thrown off, startling the eye with all sorts of shapes and colours. Here and there, perhaps, a bullock or a donkey shares the verandah with an unconscious sleeper, who snores a sweet farewell to your passing shout. And now the women come issuing from the doors, in gay cloths of many colours, with clinking bracelets and anklets, and silver girdles (if they can afford them) round their taper, supple waists; with bright, round, brass vessels, piled in twos or threes, or half-dozens, on their heads; and pass along in groups to draw water and gossip at the well. A little later, and the town scavengers scrape up the dust and dirt into ridges along the middle of the street; the herdsmen collect the cattle from yard and stall; and, just as the first sunbeam strikes the nut-branches upon the palm-trees that stand in rows along each thoroughfare, the earliest opening business man takes down his shutters, and, squatting himself amongst his baskets of grain, his packets of sugar-candy, his plantain bunches, his guava heaps, his cocoa-nuts, his pendant cobs of Indian corn, his pumpkins, or his little bales of cloths, begins to look about for customers, just for all the world as keenly as any civilized trafficker. And now outpour the lazier women, all the boys, all the girls, and all the babies; for as the sunbeam gets below the nut-branches down to the lower rings of the bare, brown cocoa-nut palms, the whole population of an Indian town turn out, and don't think of turning in again till bed-time, except it be to eat a little rice, ghee, and curry at dinner-time.

Shravana Belagola, the town that owns the statue, was, as I have said, about twenty miles from our starting-place, a distance, in this part of the world, with a sturdy trippler and a kindly sky, not worth mentioning; but in India, with a blazing sun overhead and a tropical horse, fiery, but soon exhausted, under saddle, twenty-five or thirty miles a day is the ordinary traveller's march. So, although we pricked our steeds pretty sharply through the town, as riders will do for their greater glory, be the town asleep or awake, we soon broke down into a trot, then into a jog, and shortly, by the time the sun burnt us in the back, into a steady walk, destined to be our pace for the remainder of the journey. And thus onward, over gently swelling hill and level plain, with blue mountains in the distance and a flashing sky above—onward, through fields of rice and raggy, growing ripe and yellow; by fields of tall millet and taller maize, bending with full, fat ears; by neat-looking, chessboard-like vegetable gardens, rich in all sorts of fragrant savoury pot-herbs and creeping gourd-vines; along the borders of large lakes, covered with the white and red cups of the lotus, and alive with teal and wild duck; in the shadows of the long-limbed, many-trunked banyan, the thick-foliaged tamarind, and the Persian tulip-tree, as gay as a May-day garland; over lengthy swells of stunted bush; through groves of date palms, each palm having hung about its pierced trunk a little pitcher, into which runs the toddy much beloved by coolies and thirsty travellers. Onward, by gardens of huge-leaved plantains, all tattered and torn; lofty, golden-fruited mango and strange jack-fruit trees; skirting wide tracts of the dark-green, rustling sugar-cane and mulberry plantations; diving into jungle depths of crowded forest-growth and underwood, all bound together into a mass of rank greenery by a network of verdant creepers inlaid with brilliant blossoms. Slowly onward, over the brown highway—not too well repaired,— meeting lines of pack oxen and crowds of asses laden with corn-sacks; overtaking and quickly passing waggons piled high with cotton bales, or filled with areca-nut bags; turning round the corner of a wood, and coming with a pretty surprise upon a group of chatting, laughing village girls washing the household linen amongst the reeds and water-lilies of a shady pool. Onward, keeping company for a while with a troop of mounted irregulars, in long red tunics, huge belts of white cloth, and huger turbans, armed with sword and taper lance; salaaming, as we pass him, to some native official in his palanquin of crimson cloth and yellow fringe, on his way, most likely, to see why the ryots, poor, patient, penniless ploughmen, have not paid up the land-tax. Onward, by the thick thorn fence of the village itself, catching sight of women at the mill, women pounding rice in mortars, women weaving, women spinning—none but women; the younger men being away in the fields gathering in the harvest, the sage old grandfathers assembled in a knot beneath the village fig-tree, consulting how best to obfuscate the official coming in the gold and crimson palanquin. Onward still, listening to the cooing love-notes of the doves, watching the kites sailing in slow, large circles far up in the sky, startling a herd of spotted antelopes, disturbing the philosophic meditations and earnest fishery of long-legged crane and big-billed pelican, striking with our whips at cobras wriggling across the road, laughing at the grotesquerie of monkeys in the fruit trees, blessing the white ants that dot and honeycomb the roads with heaps and holes. Onward! No; off a little bit here, at the town of Barnavara, to get a drink of milk, give the horses a handful of boiled grain in their nose-bags, and pay a visit to the big old gun—about the biggest gun I ever saw, fully twenty feet long—which the simple people have turned into a god (*linga*), and worship with fruit sacrifices, flower garlands, and rich anointings. A deified eighty-four-pounder! A case of "cannonization" with a vengeance. Onward again, over the dam of an immense tank, twelve miles round and deep enough for alligators; onward, by the cave cell of a Mussulman hermit, himself standing on the summit of the hill, at the foot of which is his dismal dwelling-place, shouting his prayers towards the holy city; onward, straight ahead, through and by all sorts of things, people and places, right into the middle of the day, by which time we reached Shravana Belagola.

Now, it happened to be the town market day, and as we wanted to see the people on a little matter of business, as well as the statue, we passed through gate (most Hindoo towns have, at least, a mud wall round them by way of fortification, and some two or three gateways) and street to the market-place, a long narrow shed covered in with red tiles, with an extensive piece of cleared ground in front. Some two or three thousand buyers and sellers, mostly seated on the ground—the wares being there also,—were haggling, as none but Easterns can haggle, over little heaps of rice, little heaps of forla, torla, hurrilee, girrilee, and other strange grains, little heaps of vegetables, very little heaps of spices and of chilli-powder, little pots of ghee, little cakes of pigments for painting the caste marks on brow and cheek, little piles of little gods for the next feast, little bundles of betel-leaf, all to be bought and sold for the very smallest coins that mint ever made. Everything little but the noise, and that was of Babel dimensions. If a man wanted half a farthing's-worth of butter, he flung his arms about, snapped his fingers, danced and screamed to the topmost pitch of his voice. So they did all of them—the whole two thousand! What with the hubbub, the heat, the dust, and the chilli, it was—well, not a pleasant halting-place after a warm ride. We managed, however, to spend an hour or two among the crowd, doing the work we had to do. Then, after shaking down a bundle of grass for our horses, we went into the shed and discussed the visit to Gomuta Roya, the stone giant on the hill. We could see his Monstership very plainly from our resting-place, rising head, shoulders, and elbows above the temple court, in the centre of which he stood; in fact, we had seen him on his mountain summit for miles before we reached the town—a Titan warder, on the look out from his watch-tower. The hill itself, Indra-Betta, an isolated cone of gneis, presented on the side towards us a perfectly bare surface, very smooth-looking and very steep, while about the base were scattered immense, boulder-shaped blocks. A little more than half a mile from Indra-Betta, uprose Chandra-giri, the moon mountain, another conical hill, and between the two nestled the town.

And now for the ascent! After resting for half an hour we started on the enterprise, taking care, first, to buy ourselves a stout bamboo each. The hill was not far from us, but at every step we took the sides of Indra-Betta seemed to grow more and more slippery and steep, till, by the time we had reached the foot, the slope, if slope it was, took on the appearance of a huge, towering, highly polished wall, slightly, very slightly, inclined from the perpendicular. To increase our sense of difficulty if not of danger, at our first step upward, half a dozen "guides" rushed forward, and seizing us by the arms, insisted on affording us their not-to-be-done-without assistance. Plainly we had before us a bit of Mont Blanc without the fissures, the avalanches, and the freezing. Freezing! The blazing sun had heated Indra-Betta to well-nigh frying point. Here was a fresh trouble; we trembled for our boots. However, there was nothing for it but a climb; so, grasping firmly our stout bamboos, we set off. They did us good service; we stuck them in every crack and crevice we could find; we bent them nearly double with our weight. The guides, too, poked and pulled at us most vigorously. When we came to a place more like a pane of glass than usual, they griped us galvanically, and begged our "most serene lordships" would "not fall, for the sake of the three worlds." When we stopped a bit to pant and rest on a ledge two or three inches wide, they told us tales of horrid headlong smashes that had happened to adventurous climbers who would have no guides. When we took off our boots to give us a better hold upon the rock, they kindly put them on their stockingless feet.

After an hour's puffing, pushing, and perspiring, we happily reached a flight of steps that led up to the summit. Now it was comparatively easy work—something like going up two or three London monuments. We dragged ourselves up as fast as we could, reached level ground at last, passed in through the temple gate, and found ourselves at the feet of the Roya—literally at his feet, for the crown of our hats scarcely reached above the giant's ankle. There he was, full seventy feet in height, stout withal, and well proportioned. The iron Achilles of Hyde Park Gate might have stood babywise upon his shoulder. He had no toga or any drapery, but a delicate creeper, springing from his heel, grew up about his huge limbs, and hung down here and there in graceful festoons, beautifully relieving the immensity of the figure itself. But the head chiefly attracted our attention. Though as gigantic as the rest, from the regular symmetry of the features, the diminution of size by the distance, enabling the eye to take in the whole face at once, and the wonderful delicacy of the work, it looked perfectly natural; while a smile, a thorough kindly, human smile, cunningly wrought in about the dimpled valleys of the mouth, seemed to endue the mighty monolith with heart and soul. Nowhere else in India can anything similar be seen. The image gods of the Hindoos are generally neither remarkable for size, grace, grandeur, nor amiability of expression. On the contrary, they are either hideous or unmeaning. Here, however, was a face that, if found near old Nile, would need no veil before Sphynx or Memnon. If Layard had been with us he would have been sorely tempted to add the Jain god to his winged bulls of Nineveh. But in vain would it be for him or any other gatherer of old-world works to attempt the deportation of Gomuta Roya, for he stands one with his mountain pedestal, the summit of the cone having been cut away till he was fairly quarried out.

We stayed perhaps about an hour, wandering in and out among the huge ten toes, calculating the probable force of a kick, speculating on the period of the giant's birth, wondering at the skill and labour of the sculptor, the tiny hand that chipped down the mountain; asking the guide how it was the Roya looked so white, learning that once a year a scaffold was erected, on which some fifty men scrubbed his highness from top to toe; tracing his shadow stretching far upon the plain; guessing at his weight, at his stride, at the results of a lightning stroke, at the effect of an earthquake, at the possibility of his large fingers some day serving the utilitarian purpose of electric wire posts, or the whole man himself becoming a beacon for the ships of some remote age, when perchance the Indian Ocean shall have washed and worn its way to the base of Indra-Betta.

Having got through all that amount of wonderment, we addressed ourselves to the task of getting down—not by any means an easy task. Still we did it, never mind how. On returning to the shed, a beggar, pitying our tired and generally done-up condition, rushing forward, unwound a cotton handkerchief from his head, and stretching it to its full dimensions, with that luxuriant magnificence of gracious politeness only to be found in an eastern clime, invited us to take our ease upon it. It was our own; "its whole length and breadth and downy softness was at the entire disposal of our lordships: we might sit upon it, lie upon it, wrap it round us, make a tent of it, or a screen; in a word, use it to our perfect liking." Generous old beggar! 'Twas kind, and yet 'twas a business speculation; he got his penny by it.

The beggar was not the only good friend we had in Shravana Belagola. The town is the seat of the great Guru—High Priest—of all the southern Jains; the chief temple of the sect, the largest monastery and college, are there. Happily, during our visit, the grand functionary was at home, and being a kindly sort of a personage, he sent us a large bunch of bananas, with a request that we would give him a call next day and accept a dinner. We sent back our salaams, and said we would do ourselves the honour, etc. In the evening, partly to while away the time, mainly, however, it must be confessed, to polish up a few handsome compliments for our host, we compared notes on the semi-Buddhistic sect, the leader of which was this good Guru.

Not many generations ago, the Jains formed the prevalent religious "persuasion" in the Mysore. The Rajah was a Jain, the Polygars or nobles were Jains, and most of the people, as became good, submissive oriental subjects, were also most loyally Jains. It was a good time, a golden age, for the dumb creation on that southern table-land in those days, for the true Jain is the most perfect suppressor of cruelty possible. Animal life, let it be enshrined in the ugliest or minutest of forms, is as sacred to him as the life of man. So far does he carry his views on this subject, that all burnt-offerings are as abominations to him, as insects crawling upon the fuel, or falling into the flame, cannot fail to be destroyed by every oblation.

Tailors, however, are not so well cared for, as, by another doctrine of the sect, the professors were enjoined to become *Diganabararu*, or sky-clad,—a very simple, inexpensive style of costume, demanding in its construction neither wool, cotton, silk, thread, thimble, or, in fact, anything else. Time, however, that father of new fashions, among other changes has altered this singular mode, so that in the present day the Jain only assumes his celestial garments, and throws off all others, at meal times.

Barbers, also, were in the background in those good old days; the priests, at least, would neither touch nor be touched by razor or scissors. Yet they were not permitted to wear a solitary hair, poor fellows! The result was that every individual "rooted sorrow" had to be plucked out from scalp, cheek, lip, eyebrow, and chin.

Curious people those Jains. Perhaps it was not a bad thing for the Mysore that such fantastic fellows were not permitted to keep their supremacy very long.

There is a strange story told about the manner in which the tide of rule began to turn with them. Some three hundred years ago, a certain Rajah of this region was anxious to ascertain the exact time when the new moon would make her appearance; why, I cannot tell: most likely he wished some fast week quickly over. Reason or no reason, his royal mind was troubled; so he summoned to his presence the priests of his domain. The good men came trooping to the solemn conclave, and after sage consultations, references to almanac tables, and mysterious reckonings, announced to the lord of many more worlds than there are that the young moon would bend her silver bow on the 1st of April. This, however, did not satisfy the royal conscience, or, taking our supposition about the fast to be true, did not meet the demands of the royal appetite; so the heretical Brahmins were called in to give their opinion. Now, as it was impossible that Brahmins and Jains should agree on any point whatsoever, the former promptly decided that the 1st of April was altogether out of the question, and that the moon, if she knew her place, would most decidedly appear on the 31st of March. Here was a pretty piece of perplexity for his Highness! He was not, however, long in coming to a decision. Being a perfectly irresponsible governor, and able to do just what he pleased, he announced to the rival pundits that the fate of each party should depend upon the truth of its prediction. "If," said he to the Jains, "you are right, you may pound the Brahmins to death in your rice mortars; and if," said he, turning to the latter, "you are right, you may, if you please, squeeze the Jains to death in the oil-presses."

Highly summary chief magistrates were those old Rajahs!

Now, to tell the truth, the Brahmins were in the wrong, and this they knew only too well; they believed in the 1st of April as much as the others, but it was, of course, utterly out of the question that they should adhere to the same day as their rival religionists. The 1st of April being an undisputed fact, these unfortunates were put to their wits' end how to escape the rice mortars. Could Chandra be induced to quicken her pace a little? What about a pale sort of fire balloon? A thousand schemes were suggested, and set aside as worthless. At last it was agreed that Agnee, the god of fire, should be included in their councils, and be petitioned to assist his servants in their need. Forthwith they chanted holy, mighty incantations—words of magic power over the very gods; sacrifices of flowers and fruit were severally offered, fasts were commenced and penances inflicted, till, moved by such zealous devotion, the propitiated deity nodded compliance from the Hindoo Olympus. Great was the joy of the grateful men; there was to be no more fear of poundings for them, but ecstatic visions of Jain-squeezing in the oil-mills. Agnee would help them; they might swear to the 31st with the confidence of truth. The other honest folk, knowing nothing of the fire-god's intention, and trusting to their almanac, were quite as triumphant.

Already had they marked down in white chalk the 1st of April to be kept for ever by all good Jains as a glorious memory. At last March, that windiest of months, blew himself into the last day. The 31st came. Up blazed the sun into the zenith, looking as if he neither knew nor cared to know whether there was a moon at all. All the change that the story says flitted across his flashing face, was a slight astonishment to see so many people on the Mysore plains all gazing skyward, and yet not seeming to be on the look-out for him.

Yes, there they were, shaved Brahmins and polled

Jains; the former anxiously, notwithstanding Agnee's promise, the latter sarcastically, peering into the blue depths long before the point of decision could possibly arrive. The day wore on; the sun went down with a sulky, lowering look as the crowds of gazers kept their backs to him, still looking eastward though he was not there, and would not be for many a long hour. At last the time came, the very minute; more than a million eyes strained into the depths of the gloaming, the watchers scarcely breathed, the Jains ceased their scoffing, the Brahmins fell on their knees. The final second pulsed through the veins of Time, when, at first faint and pale, then clear and bright, the silver curve drew itself on nature's huge blackboard. "Chandra! Chandra! The moon! the moon!" thundered forth the triumphant Brahmins, while the unlucky Jains, in amazed grief, went off to the oil-mills. And squeezed they were, for the Brahmins hated them to the hottest point of persecution. For many a day and month and year, the huge, creaking mills were horribly busy, and ran red with blood till the Jains almost ceased in the land; the few thousands that remained seeking shelter in Shravana Belagola, deeming themselves secure within the shadow of Gomuta Roya, the stone giant on the hill.

די

THE GURU'S DINNER.

Having received an invitation to dinner from the Guru, or High Priest of the Jains, my friend and I started about two o'clock the next day, to pay our respects to his Sanctity. At the entrance to the courtyard of his monastery, we were very solemnly received by three or four novices, who conducted us to a raised verandah formed along three sides of a quadrangle about a hundred feet square, and out of which about twenty or thirty doors opened into as many apartments, and these again into others; but as we were not permitted to enter the main building, I can say no more about its interior arrangements. In the verandah into which we were introduced, there were three chairs and a table. We seated ourselves just opposite a dark-looking staircase, down which we expected our host would come.

After a few seconds a young *shishyaru*, or student, approaching on tiptoe, whispered to us that the great man was asleep. We knew at once that we should have to wait till the nap was over, as it is an unpardonable crime to wake a Hindoo. After sitting in silent admiration of each other for five minutes, we walked round the quadrangle in search of some feature of interest, and fortunately discovered that one side, sheltered by a deep verandah roof, was covered with paintings done in a style sufficiently quaint to make a pre-Raphaelite mad with despair. What struck us most was the wonderful way in which the cunning artist had managed to give to view the secrets of nature. A river, for instance, formed a part of the picture; accordingly the clever fellow had first streaked along the wall a line of green for the off bank, then a broad line of blue for the water; then beneath the blue he had put in a long heap of fish, next an underlying stratum of unfortunate drowned men, then a pavement of shells, then a brown strip of mud, then a yellow ditto of sand, and finally another green line, to represent the near bank. While we were looking admiringly at this bit of Jain taste, preparations had been going on in the neighbourhood of the three chairs. One sombre-looking disciple had brought in a silver snuff-box and placed it on the table, another, with a sense of awful responsibility in his face, deposited a cuscus fan, and a third was busy adjusting the Guru's chair at a suitable conversational angle when we left the picture on the wall and returned to our seats. Scarcely had we sat down, when two naked black feet appeared on the pre-mentioned staircase; half a second, and the feet were followed by two very big black knees; gradually the borders of a piece of drapery discovered itself, then a whole bundle of cloth girdled about a fine Falstaffian waist; after which came shining black shoulders, and last of all, a big, bullet-shaped head, bare, unctuous, and hairless. It was the Guru. We rose, salaamed, bowed at an angle of 90 degrees; he did the same. We sat down, so did he; and then we bandied compliments for half an hour, calling each other the pleasantest names possible. Then we discussed the whole range of everything, in a style as compendious as the subject. After which the great man undid his legs, which he had tied up in a knot beneath him on his chair, after the manner of the East, salaamed graciously, and returned to his staircase. For although his Guruship had invited us to dinner, he could not by any means dine with us, we being, in an ethnological point of view, a tolerable sort of chimpanzee to his manhood; in the social scale, dust to his ponderosity; and, in a religious look-out, nothing whatever to his everything. We, however, being of John Company's caste, he would give us a meal though he would not mess with us. Yet we were not served worse than the Governor-General would have been, had he stopped and dined at the *Mertha* of Shravana Belagola.

The place to which we were conducted was outside the monastery,—it was, in fact, a detached, solitary room, with one side entirely open to the street; inside, we found a table and a couple of chairs. We walked in and made ourselves at home. Shortly after, a disciple came with a huge cloth, with which he screened us from the public gaze. After a minute, a corner of the drapery was raised, and a young priest brought in a couple of immense banana leaves, glazed with melted sugar; these were to be our plates. A large quantity of boiled rice followed, in a neatly made dish of the same material, accompanied by curry, chetney, pickles, and sauces in endless variety and of volcanic intensity of heat, all served up in leaf cups of greater or less size. Three or four priests placed themselves round the hospitable board, ready to wait upon us. "Very good," we said to each other; "but where are the knives, the forks, the spoons? How are we to get these things on our plates?" The question was soon answered. Two black hands went up to the wrists in the rice-dish and threw their contents down on our plates; a couple more did the same kind office with the curry; long black fingers dropped pieces of pickle and pinches of chetney on the smoking mess. Thus the carving was done; and now we had to use our fingers, which we did with a vigour of execution that perfectly astonished us.

We said to ourselves afterwards, "That man is contemptible who is dependent on Birmingham and Sheffield for his dinner, and he who cannot eat without cutlery and crockery-ware deserves to starve." The serious duties of the meal being over, our polite attendants, having first poured water upon our curry-stained fingers, brought us fresh milk in brass goblets for our refreshment. And hereupon another "custom" stepped in to puzzle us. No Hindoo touches with his lips the vessel he drinks from; he raises it to about a foot from his upturned face, and skilfully directs the stream into his opened mouth. Now, this was an exploit which we had often admired, but which we felt ourselves utterly unable to perform. Yet we were unwilling to forego the pleasures and excitements of the milk jug; so, placing our hands together, after the manner of little boys about to get a "lot" of sweetmeats, we received the milk in our hollow palms, and drank long draughts to our hearts' content. Plantains, oranges, mangoes, and guavas completed our repast. The veil was withdrawn, we made our bow to the novices, sent our compliments to his Sanctity, mounted our horses, and cantered out of Shravana Belagola, with the shadow of the Jain giant god upon our path.

WHAT HAS ENGLAND DONE FOR INDIA?

A Lecture delivered in Grahamstown, 1856.

In considering this subject we must be careful to select a right starting-point. It is now many years since Alderman Goddard, in the golden days of Queen Bess, gave a dinner to some brother merchants in the City, to talk over the matter of an adventure to the Indies. We can scarcely begin with that dinner. Much was said, we doubt not, about bales of silk, boxes of spicery, diamonds from Golconda, pearls from Ceylon, muslins from Dacca, shawls from Cashmere, good ships with overflowing holds, wharves crowded with strange wealth, stores piled high and bursting, strong boxes full of golden dividends: plenty of talk we may be sure there was about such things, and I hope they got them. I hope Alderman Goddard grew rich, was knighted, was made Lord Mayor, and married his daughter to an earl's son. Yet it is plain, to begin with this dinner will not answer our purpose.

In due time these good merchants obtained a charter with the Queen's name and the state seal all glorious at the bottom, and forthwith they sent out writers and servants, trusty and true, to the shores of Coromandel, who, in the name of their masters, partly bought, partly begged, and partly borrowed, a foot or two of land on which to build a store. They called it a factory.

I am afraid the factory is no better starting-point than the dinner. Should we commence here we should have to tell a long tale of British skill at bargain-striking, British devotion to the main point, the wonderful elasticity of British treaties, the terrible tenacity of the British grip, the miraculous capacity of the British swallow. The Company's mill was most liberal; everything was "grist" that came to it: pearls and princes, cloves and crowns, sugar and subjects, rice and rubies.

The charter displayed more magical power than the lamp of Aladdin. Under its influences factories bristled up into forts; quiet clerks pored o'er their ledgers over-night, dreamt of invoices, and woke up next morning grim fighting men; grey goose-quills hardened, lengthened, and sharpened themselves into swords; pounce-bags were rounded off into hot and heavy-cannon balls, and traffic, an old, and as everybody thought, honest word, gradually, letter by letter, changed itself into war, then into conquest, and has latterly come to call itself annexation. No, it will not do to begin with the factory.

On the 19th day of October, 1774, nearly 200 years from the establishment of the first Company, and by which time the power of the French (glorious allies now, but terrible enemies then) and the Dutch had been broken in the East, the war in the Deccan finished, Gheria destroyed, the horrors of the Black Hole of Calcutta avenged by the sack of Hooghly and the battle of Plassey, Chandernagore taken, Mir Jaffier made puppet Nabob, Omichund deceived and ruined by the forgery of Clive, the Nabob of Oude defeated, the Great Mogul pensioned, the Sunyasi hordes cut up and the Rohillas vanquished, the Company's possessions in India were united under a Governor-Generalship.

Scarcely had Warren Hastings seated himself on the Company's musnud than he was obliged, by the peculiar fatality which has ever attended our rule in India, to enter upon the stormy and puzzling sea of Mahratta politics, and the endless marchings and counter-marchings of Mahratta war. He had to fight his own council, to hang Nuncomar, to do long and doubtful battle with Hyder Ali. He had to fill an empty treasury, and travel all the way to Benares to dun an unwilling Rajah; had to suppress a revolt, set up a new chief, and commission Asoph-ul-Dowla to hunt up and seize the hidden treasures of the celebrated begums of Oude.

This was doing a great deal to preserve and extend the British Empire in the East, but it would be difficult to discover in this entangled web of intrigue and war the golden thread of social improvement. In fact, almost up to the beginning of the present century the great question with the Company was not what shall we do *for* India, but how shall we get it, and then how shall we keep it.

From that early day, when the United Company of Merchants gave up business, and retired into the peaceful privacy of the council-room and the camp, they were compelled, to use the language of polite history, by the necessities and responsibilities of their position, to go to war with almost every prince and race in the continent. That was their mission, and they accepted it with a willingness, and carried it out with a success that at least demands admiration, and might very well excite envy on the frontier of Kaffirland. What could be done for a country that was undergoing the bitter pangs of invasion, conquest, and seizure throughout almost every square mile of its mountain, valley, and broad plain? It is known right well and painfully, here as much as anywhere, that civilization, the grace and glory of life, will not flourish on the war trail.

And even within the period we have selected as the time of better things, India has enjoyed no lasting season of rest. For thirteen years, from 1786 to 1800, the whole of South India was disorganized by the war with Tippoo Sultan. Then followed a fresh Mahratta war, then the war with the Nepaulese, then the war with the Pindarees, then the war with the Burmese, then the war with the Affghans, then the war in Sindh, then the war with Gwalior, then the first war with the Sikhs, then the Multan outbreak, then the second war with the Sikhs, and then the second war with the Burmese.

During the last sixty years, twenty great historic battles have been fought on the soil of India, besides fights and skirmishes innumerable; twelve celebrated fortresses have been captured, a hundred mountain fastnesses have been scaled and dismantled, and no less than five renowned military races have been overcome, humbled, broken up, and, in some instances, gathered into the ranks of our own army.

We could not therefore rationally expect that, parallel with this series of wars, there should be a series of grand internal improvements for me, or any one, to relate.

Nevertheless there have been improvements, and, in spite of unfavourable influences, they are neither few nor small.

Suppose, at any time—say somewhere about the reign of Henry VIII., and for centuries before that—it was and had been the custom in England to bind together in one winding-sheet, and place together in one coffin, and burn together in one funeral pile, the living and the dead, and suppose the horrid custom suddenly and for ever abolished by law, should we not value that law at a price equal at least to that of Magna Charta? If so, then we must carry that valuation to the credit side of the Company's rule, which, in 1830, abolished Sutteeism in India.

Suppose, again, that about the same time thousands of British mothers were in the habit of yearly pilgrimage to the Thames to cast their infants into its waters, and add to that horror the crocodiles of Saugur, and suppose that custom suddenly and at once ended by law, should we not set greater store by that law than we do by the Bill of Rights? If so, there is another item to be put down to the Company's credit, under the style of infanticide abolished in India. And if about the same time it was a common thing in any part of England to bind hand and foot, torture horribly, and slay a hundred men or so about sowing time and harvest, and if that rite were suddenly and for ever put an end to by law, should not we think Reform Bills nothing by the side of such a law? If so, the Company gains by that; for its Governors-General have put down human sacrifices in India, and the Toda now slays his fat buffalo, when formerly the unhappy Burger would have been the victim.

Suppose, once more, a widely scattered race of men, bound to silence, secrecy, and mutual fidelity by oaths and fearful ceremonies, haunted every highway, lay hid in the shades of every forest, ready and eager to strangle, just for the mere love and pleasure of strangling, and suppose the whole race of murderers hunted up, discovered, and destroyed, would not the day on which that was done be more memorable than any 10th of April that England was ever saved from? If so, the Company gains again; for within the last dozen years it has rooted out, shut up in prisons, or sent to work upon the roads, the whole community of Thugs.

The Company cannot be considered insolvent while it has those four abolished horrors posted on the right side of the historic ledger.

But the Government has not been satisfied with abolishing evils, it has undoubtedly conferred on the people of India many positive benefits.

In the important particular of the administration of justice a considerable advance has been made on the old Hindoo or Mohammedan law practice. A Delhi native paper furnishes satisfactory evidence on this point. "Formerly," it says, "the city was unsafe after sunset, now it is quite secure. Formerly no man dared to travel in the jungle without a guard, now the loneliest traveller has no fear. Under native rulers justice was put up to sale, but under British rule all obtain equal justice, and religious scruples are respected." So far goes the testimony of a Hindoo, and he might have added to his list of contrasts that there is no longer in the state any power that can order, under the influence of a gust of passion, the meanest labourer to be trampled to death by elephants, as was once the case. As in England, so now in India, the poorest in the land are as much under the protection of the law as the highest and the wealthiest.

It will give us more definite notions of the benefits, administrative and social, conferred by British rule in India, if we confine our attention for five minutes to what has been done in a single province of the country.

I select the Mysore, as that is the part of Hindostan in which I have been resident for the last nine years.

The Mysore is not strictly a part of the Company's possessions; it is, however, to all intents and purposes, under British control. Its Rajah is a state prisoner, confined to a circle of some dozen miles around his palace, and receives, unfortunate man, the miserable pittance of £140,000 a year. The entire government is administered by English officers in subordination to the Governor-General of India. Let me speak of this country as it was before it came under British influence. In 1761 it was ravaged by the Mahrattas under Bunnee Visagee; in 1765 (four years afterwards), in 1767 (two years after that), in 1770, after a three years' interval, it was ravaged by the Peshwar Madhurar; in 1771, after a protracted peace of six months, it was laid waste by Tembuck Row, four years afterwards by Ragonauth Row, two years after that by Hurry Punt, ten years after that by the same chief, five years after that by the Peishwa, and one year after that by Purseram Row. Thus in thirty years it suffered ten invasions; not mere frontier attacks, but genuine invasions, carried right through the heart and body of the country—real crop trampling, forage wasting, cattle destroying, town and village burning, women and children slaying invasions, from men more cruel than Kaffirs and more deceitful than Hottentots.

Then, added on to these Mahratta raids and wholesale slaughterings, were the Hyder and Tippoo wars, and their worse rule.

Hyder was an ignorant and bigoted Mussulman usurper, who, with the cunning of a common thief, and the brutality of a brigand, wriggled and fought his way to the Mysore throne, and then ruled his subjects with the sword.

His son Tippoo was a monster of cruelty. His name meant Tiger, and his nature justified his name. His tastes, propensities, and pleasures were all tigerish. It is said that "he called his soldiers his tigers of war. The tigers of the jungle were his pets, and often his executioners; for the attendant who offended him, or the prisoner who was brought into his presence, was not unfrequently turned into a barred room, or large cage, where the savage animals were let loose upon him. Near the door of his treasury an enormous tiger was found chained, when his palace was taken. Other tigers were in the edifice at the same time." A big toy invented for the amusement of this sultan tells the whole story of his character and life. It was a rude automaton tiger, killing and about to devour a man. It is now one of the sights of the East India House, Leadenhall Street.

Frequently have I talked with old Hindoos who were children in the days of Tippoo the Tiger, and heard them whisper stories of his cruelties in bated breath; how that by thousands he would force Hindoos to become Mohammedans, bathe Brahmins in the blood of their sacred bulls, build horrid prisons of rank mud, slime, dead serpents, toads, and scorpions, in the midst of pestiferous jungles, and do other deeds that I would not like to tell or you to hear.

These men ruled the Mysore just forty years.

Then came the present Maharajah, Krishna Oudiar. He was but a boy of six when he was taken from his hiding-place in a village and exalted to a throne, under the protection of the British Government. During his minority, the kingdom was well governed, first under the late Duke of Wellington (then Colonel Wellesley), afterwards by the Dewan Pooniah. But as soon as the Rajah came of age, he threw off the control of wisdom and experience, entered on a career of wasteful extravagance and gross pleasures, made councillors of buffoons, companions of dancing girls, and gods of idle Brahmins; emptied his treasury in a few years, and, to replenish it, sold whole provinces to the highest bidders, took bribes with both hands, and rack-rented his entire kingdom. The usual results followed; the oppressed peasantry, irritated beyond endurance, broke out into rebellion, hanged on a hundred trees the Brahmin middle men who had helped to wrong them, and committed all the well-known excesses of agrarian revolt.

Then came the suppression in due course, and terrible reprisals were taken from the miserable ryots. The vengeance of the Rajah was worse than his oppression. Then it was that the Company stepped in and relieved his Highness of the burden of government, and the people from his tyranny. This happened about 1833, or little more than twenty years ago. And now let us look at the other picture.

The natural features of the country were, of course, the same before as after British rule. The whole country is a table-land, lifted up on the shoulders of the Eastern and Western Ghauts, 3000 feet above the level of the sea.

It has an area of 30,000 square miles. It is watered by forty rivers, and ten thousand lakes and reservoirs, and has a population of four millions.

Its mountain jungles are luxuriant with flowering shrubs and clustering creepers of a hundred varieties. Forests of teak, sandal-wood, ebony, wild cinnamon, and nutmeg-trees darken the slopes of the western hills, while groves of date and sago palms dot its central plains.

These were there when Tippoo reigned and when the Mahrattas ravaged. True! But its cultivated lands were not; they were laid waste, burnt over, hardened by the feet of armies, or neglected by the unwilling peasant. Now they are beautiful over a hundred square miles with rice crops, the greenest of all cereals; the tall flags of the sugar-cane rustle in every breeze that blows over the whole face of the country; while raggy, avary, tovary, jola, hurrilee, and many an Eastern grain of outlandish name help to make the Mysore the granary of surrounding countries.

Its gardens are fragrant with spice plants, and tempting with the milky cocoa-nut, the golden orange, the rosy-cheeked apple, the russet pomegranate, and the dark-green mango; strawberries blush along the borders, and trellised grape-vines bend to the ground with too much sweetness; while the guava, the custard apple, the jack-fruit, and the plantain flourish abundantly.

And what is better than this, the reason and cause of the whole, there is peace in the land—peace, justice, and heart to work. The people plough and weave, gather in the yellow silk cocoon, press out the sweet juice of the cane, buy and sell, take rich merchandise to distant market towns, no longer bury their golden "mohurs" in cunning hiding-places. They marry in the midst of music, their children saunter to the daily school, the old men die upon their beds, and have decent burial.

There are twelve educational institutions established for the purpose of teaching the natives the English tongue and literature. Government supports a model stud to give the people better horses; a model cattle farm, sheep farm, cotton farm, and silk farm; and coffee plantations are multiplying themselves on every side.

The Mysore is noted throughout India for its numerous and well-made roads, and magnificent travellers' bungalows. The electric telegraph traverses its whole length, bridges span its rivers, and, just as I left, a fussy locomotive was bursting into a whistle where not long since growled the tigers of the Sultan Tippoo.

British rule has then done something for the Mysore. And I could take you to other provinces where equally beneficial results have been wrought out by the same cause; to the Punjab, for instance, where, to quote an abstract of an Indian Blue-Book, within three years from the time of taking possession, the British Administrators have introduced as much tranquillity, order, and prosperity as is enjoyed by any other district in India. They have extinguished all the elements of internal disturbance, have converted the more martial spirits of the population into faithful soldiers of the Government, have reclaimed the others to habits of commercial industry, have commenced works of public utility on an unexampled scale, have brought much additional land under cultivation, and have so arranged the finances of the province, that though considerably less is raised from the people than under the rule of Runjeet, the present balance-sheet of the Government shows a clear annual surplus of half a million sterling.

Or I could take you to Sindh, with its thriving seaport, Kurrachee, at the mouth of the Indus, through which the produce of North Western India is now floated to the sea; and which, not a dozen years ago, when Napier took it, was altogether innocent of trade.

I cannot help fervently wishing that Kaffirland were in India! If it could, by any sleight of hand, be taken out of our neighbourhood and put down bodily anywhere between the Himalayas and Cape Comorin, within the next half a dozen years it would be comfortably annexed, three-quarters civilized, taxed up to a surplus revenue that would beat Lahore, and its brawny sons, thrust into red jackets, would be sent off to scale the walls of Sebastopol.

The things which India wants, are just what South Africa wants—water and roads; means of irrigation, and facilities for transport: the grand requisite for production, and the grand requisite for commerce.

The attention and efforts of the British Government have lately been energetically directed towards supplying these requisites. An extensive system of canal irrigation has been projected, and partly carried out.

The Western Jumna Canal was the first great work of the kind executed. It extends from the foot of the Suwalic Hills to Delhi and to Hissar. Its total length is 425 miles, and there are nearly 700 irrigation outlets from the main channel. This canal has called into being, in places formerly without an inhabitant, an active, contented, and prosperous peasantry.

The Eastern Jumna Canal, though a work of inferior proportions, has proved one of great importance and value. Its entire length is 155 miles. By these two canals the entire stream of a river, once 700 miles long, has been diverted from its course.

The next undertaking of this nature is the Great Ganges Canal, a new river made by the Company at an expense of nearly two millions sterling, and traversing nearly 1000 miles of country. Probably the most magnificent single work of human industry to be found in the world.

Another canal, of 450 miles, in the Punjab, and others in the Madras Presidency, will, in the course of a few years, add their graceful and life-giving testimony to the good of the Company's rule.

As to roads, no doubt the Company might have done better; yet the following lines of trunk road will not be thought utterly contemptible. From Calcutta to Peshawar a line of 1500 miles, from Calcutta to Bombay 1000 miles, from Bombay to Agra 800 miles, from Madras to Mangalore 500 miles; altogether a total of nearly 4000 miles of well-made roads.

But for the purposes of traffic and of life, India should have that mileage multiplied by hundreds. From a want of internal communication, it not unfrequently happens there that in one province there is a glut of food stuffs, and corn is rotting on the ground, while in another province the people are suffering all the horrors of a famine.

What has the Indian Government done in the direction of education?

To take the money view of this question first. It has for some time past set apart £45,000 a year for the purposes of public instruction.

Now £45,000 is not in itself a despicable sum, and £45,000 a year is still less so, but when contrasted with a revenue of twenty six-millions, it is a mere miser's dole ; and when given to meet the wants of one hundred million of people, a simple mockery.

Of course so small an amount could not possibly be made to meet the demands of the country. In fact, the Government evidently never intended the grant to be national, but metropolitan. The whole £45,000 has been expended on the presidency and one or two other first-rate towns, in supporting superior schools and colleges for the benefit of about a yearly average of 25,000 students.

The style of education bestowed on this select and favoured band is certainly superior. A proficient in any of the Presidency Universities is considered to be familiar with Dr. Farmer's criticism on Shakespeare, be "well up" with the politics of modern Europe, to have a head knowledge of the second and third year book, work of Cambridge mathematics, and a respectable acquaintance with Bacon and Locke.

Nor has this high intellectual course been wholly without result in a moral point of view. In all the collegiate towns there are swarms of doubters, of men who are thinking and feeling their way up out of superstition, who, it may be, are now groping about in the region of error and scepticism, but who will by-and-by reach the upper land of truth. Many old prejudices are gradually being shamed out of existence.

Medical students have been induced to forego the

national and religious horror of touching a dead body, and many of them use the scalpel with a skill equal to that of Europeans. I was very much astonished one morning at noticing the following advertisement in a newspaper— "P. Soondrum, Dentist." To any one acquainted with the habits of the Hindoos, such an announcement is startling, and very significant. In India, to declare the dentist to be abroad, would be a far more striking indication of advance than the widest travels of the schoolmaster. A Hindoo who has been induced to touch a tooth, may be at once pronounced to be civilized up to a point of almost miraculous perfection. It may seem strange that an appetite for beef-steaks should be numbered among the results of an Indian University education. Nevertheless it is so. Many of the Government students have emancipated themselves from the insipidities of a vegetable diet, and, what is better, have divested the bull of his sacred character and have publicly eaten beef.

When Tippoo Sultan's Mohammedan palace was seized by the British, his pantry was found to be well stocked with well-cured hams, but they were always carried to the pious Mussulman's table under the title of legs of mutton. The Brahmins of Northern India, who hold all life to be sacred, eat fish, and pacify their consciences by calling them marine vegetables. But the alumni of Calcutta revel unblushingly and without disguise in their newly discovered luxuries of sirloins and fat rounds.

Within the domain of English literature, educated Hindoos have highly signalized themselves.

I have read articles in the *Calcutta Review*, written by natives, equal in all respects to papers in our home quarterlies. For a long time Somachunder Dutt edited one of the ablest English newspapers in the Madras Presidency.

A year or two ago, Sham Row published an abstract of Butler's Analogy.

But the Government educational efforts, in conjunction with missionary agency, have also exerted a powerful and beneficial influence on vernacular literature. Thus the Government operations, though carried on on a narrow base, have not been altogether useless. And I am happy to say that the base is about to be widened to dimensions the most liberal.

The following is an outline of the plan upon which state education in India, according to a despatch sent by the home authorities to Calcutta, is to be carried out:—

1st. The appointment of a Minister of Public Instruction in each presidency.

2nd. The creation of universities on the plan of the London University.

3rd. The absolute equality of the upper ten thousand and the masses for whom vernacular instruction is to be supplied.

4th. The universal and formal sanction of grants in aid, without distinction of creed, and hampered by no condition except the right of the giver to watch the application of his gift.

There is nothing one-sided about the measure. On the one hand there is to be English for those who desire it, on the other the vernaculars for those who are, from position or circumstance, unambitious of the higher language; while to all, through both channels, knowledge is to flow from the purer fountains of the West.

It is no plan for converting a section of the youth of two or three large cities into the monstrosities of college hot-beds, brilliant specimens of Hindoo intellect developed under costly, special protective and exciting influences. No! To whatever elevated grade of attainment the proposed university honours are intended to attract the "senior wrangler" and "first-class men" of India, the grand educational benefits set forth in the despatch are to be distributed, in proportion graduated only by nature and condition, to the masses. Crowded, commercial, government, and seaport towns will, without doubt, take the share they do in all countries; but right into the heart of the land, wherever a village is populous enough to have a hundred children, and wise enough to wish to have a school, there is to be set up a knowledge factory. At first, perhaps, the material turned out may be inferior, but that is only a matter of time, and may be borne with patiently, in the sure conviction that improvement is inevitable. The only monopoly henceforth is that which in all climes is secured by superior skill. He is to profit most by state assistance who has the ability to do so. The Brahmin, Bahoo, and ryot, the city boy and the village lout, will alike have a right to the ladder, and the number of steps each will climb will depend on the vigour of his efforts.

In fact, this liberal educational plan, together with

certain legislative and national movements, would lead the attentive observer to the belief, that from about this present time is to be dated a new era for India. The old civilization of this country is about to come in actual contact with the comparatively new civilization of Europe. The two have, as we have seen, touched at certain points already. The higher and more sensitive humanity of the West at a comparatively early period revolted at, and placed a restraint upon, the more prominent cruelties of the East; but the whole bulk of both systems are now to come together. Whatever activities are at work at home, are henceforth to extend the circle of their operations to this country. India is to share in the agitations, the reforms, of England. Whatever shock is felt in the one shall also shake the other. The parts of the empire, though separated by oceans and continents, are to be brought together by the energetic wish of the governors to govern well, and by the newly awakened desire of the governed that they should be governed well. Both sides approach; the prayers and petitions of the people of India demand—it may be with exaggerated vehemence—what official despatches and general orders hasten to grant, only tempering their boons and redresses with the cooler and more measured formalities natural to office and authority.

Capital, sleeping in well-locked Chubbs at home, has lately been aroused by the cry of thirsty Indian lands for water, and by-and-by more river dams, huge reservoirs, and monster canals will overspread wide wastes with green fertility; new staple products are to be introduced to willing soils, and old inferior ones improved and made saleable in fastidious markets, by a better and more generous agriculture.

Even the quarrels of Europe are to work out unknown wealth for the East, and on the ruins of Russian trade India is to found another commerce.

Though without a prophet's mantle, I may, I think, venture to say that now is the beginning of a new India. Worn out by age, new elements, imparted by another nation in its prime of vigour, are to exchange its dotage for a second infancy. And we may hope that the people of that country will pass from death to life without agony, though seldom is national regeneration quietly worked out. Not to go to the lands of Europe, where revolutions are as bloody as they are abortive, China near at hand is at this moment a terrible instance of change perfected by agonizing convulsions and terrific horrors. But while native reform associations and young Bengal clubs wax indignant over wrongs, and fling out invectives against British rule, let them know that the wrongs they deplore would have existed, under aggravated forms, under any other power, but that under no other power would they obtain redress without fierce struggle and bitter suffering.

THE INDIAN CATASTROPHE.

Written in 1857.

Since 1639, when a strip of land about the size of a South African sheep farm formed the Company's chief possession in India, up to the present day, when the Eastern Empire stretches itself from the Arabian Sea, over peninsula and bay to the swamps of the Irrawadi, no calamity has befallen British sway so terrible as the tragedy of Delhi and the north-west, the whole horrors of which we have yet to learn. The wholesale murder in the Black Hole of Calcutta, where a hundred and twenty-three Englishmen were crowded together to death in a single night; the terrors of the dungeons of Tippoo Sultan, in which British soldiers underwent nameless cruelties; the slaughter of our troops by the mutineers of Vellore; and the fearful disasters of the Affghan passes, will seem fair pages in our Indian histories in comparison with the story of their last dishonouring reverse.

The originating causes of the catastrophe cannot be absolutely decided on at present, while all energies are engaged in the stern work of suppression and retribution;

yet, from facts that have come to light in the glare of the irruption itself, taken together with other facts which have had an observable significance for some time past, sufficient indications of the probable causes have been afforded to guide us at least to an opinion.; especially when these facts are considered in connection with the antecedents and characters of the Indian races, certain analogous events in Indian history, and the constitution of the Indian army.

Putting together the following particulars supplied by the summaries of the Eastern newspapers—the Mohammedan complexion of the area of disturbance, the complicity of the late King of Oude, the discovered documents according to which Calcutta was to be divided among the Mohammedan followers of that dethroned prince and the local Mussulmans, the manifesto of the Fyzabad Moulvee, the Persian couplets of the Fakir Niamutoslah, and the elevation of a descendant of the Moguls to the throne of India on the one side—and on the other, the revolt of the Hindoo sepoys unaccompanied by any outbreak of the Hindoo people—we are led to the conclusion that the movement is rebellious as far as it is Mohammedan and mutinous as far as it is Hindoo; and that it is thus traceable to widely different causes—probably to a national turbulence and an unsuppressed desire after the ancient supremacy on the part of the Mohammedans, excited by recent events such as the annexation of Oude; and, on the part of the Hindoos, to some grievance, very likely the "fat in the cartridge," and to some serious defects in the organization of the army of which they formed a part.

When we took possession of India it was just as much Mohammedan as it is now British. The provinces of the Mogul Empire, disunited by the invasion of the Persian Nadir Shah, in the middle of the 18th century, were erected into so many Mohammedan principalities, the seats of so many Mohammedan thrones, which we, at intervals of greater or less length, have industriously overthrown—the last upset being that which Lord Dalhousie accomplished but yesterday at Lucknow. Our strife for conquest and possession has been not so much with Hindoos as with Mohammedans. The relative position in which we found the two races is analogous to that which hunters tell us of, who have seen in our African wilds the giraffe struggling and panting beneath the fangs and claws of a lion. We secured or knocked off the lion and put both him and his victim into our *menagerie;* and in so doing won for ever the hate of his disappointed majesty, who since that day has crouched sulkily, watching for opportunity over his paws. Scarcely anywhere has the Mohammedan taken kindly to our rule, acquiesced in altered conditions, and endeavoured to accommodate himself to the changes consequent on the introduction of European elements into government, society, and laws. Proud and overbearing by nature, warlike by hereditary endowment, exclusive and bigoted by religion, he keeps himself aloof, sowing his isolation with memories of a rule when by virtue of his beard, the terror of his sword, and the favour of Allah he was lord over many slaves, many plains, many mountains, many rivers, and many cities; surrounding himself to the utmost of his ability with mementos, even if but mockeries of the past. The pensioned Nabob, Nizam or king, keeps up within the high walls that jealously enclose his residence, the miserable and ghostly semblance of a court, in which sham soubadhars, grand viziers, and councillors prostrate themselves before sham thrones; has his state elephants, his state horses, his state palkee, houdah, and sword, his seraglios and eunuchs, his buffoons and dwarfs, his tigers and cheetahs, his tawdry body-guard, and more tawdry equipages; debauches himself despotically, corrupts whole neighbourhoods, as his august fathers before him ravaged nations; revels in an expenditure as reckless as if his revenues were yet collected by armies; and keeps flowing beneath all an undercurrent of conspiracy. And the same pretentious spirit animates all ranks, down to the lordly owner of £2 a month, who calls his mud hut a "Dewankhan," or royal palace, buys a shambling pony, gorgeously arrays it in a cast-off crimson saddle cloth, rides forth attended by a half-dozen ragged retainers, fancies himself Baber, Akbar, Aurungzebe, and Koole Khan going forth to conquer, and lives upon the skin of his teeth. We have ourselves a vivid recollection of a black-bearded, whiteturbaned moolah who, having invested half his property in the purchase of a gold-headed cane, was wont to stretch it out and wave it generally over this Hindoo community, saying, "What are we? Are we not sent to possess and punish these people?"

In the south of India, the locality of our experience, the Mussulman, by his proud reminiscences, his sullen temper, and slower nature, keeps himself out of the walks of life in which now alone honour and emolument can be found; the Hindoo, subtle, plastic, and insinuating, has made his way in court-house and counting-house, while the Mussulman, when driven by his necessities to seek employment, buckles on the peon's belt, runs at the stirrup of his master, or enlists, to grumble and conspire in a Company's regiment. The same causes, in part, shut him out of the government and other educational institutions of the country. In the territory once governed by Hyder Ali and Tippoo Sultan, and thick with Mussulmans to this day, in a school containing 200 boys there were but three Mohammedans; and in another, numbering 300 students, there were but five, two of whom were the sons of Persian horse-dealers, hangers-on upon the market; while it has only been within the last half a dozen years that Dr. Balfour has been able to persuade the Nabob of the Carnatic to establish a school for the benefit of 30,000 Mohammedans of Madras. Elsewhere, in this and perhaps in other respects, conditions may be modified, but nowhere so as to elevate the 20,000,000 of the faithful (supposed to be the number of Mohammedans in British and Native India) above the status of a people who belong more to the Tartar past than to the British present; and who would rejoice in any change that would put back the dial of Indian life and rule to the time of Sultan Baber when Lahore, Moultan, Ajmere, Delhi, Agra, Allahabad, Bahar, Oude, Bengal, Malwa, and Guzerat were so many centres from which the conquering hosts carried the green flag and the crescent from the Indus to the Ganges, and from the banks of both downwards to the Cauvery. Just the very people are they to remain through centuries jealous of a race that had supplanted them, to be eager after replacement, and to seize at once upon an opportunity to strike, whether that opportunity be afforded to them by the intrigues of their own princes, or the disaffection of a native army, or both happening together.

The Hindoos present very contrary characteristics to the Mohammedans. They seem to bear some resemblance to their own oxen who, with necks curved downward and shoulder surmounted and padded with the hump, seem made for the yoke.

India is not all British, but everywhere in India the Hindoos submit. At Pondicherry they bow down to the tricolour, swear by Louis Napoleon, speak French through their noses, carry their quarrels and causes to the court of *première juridiction*, acquire the secrets of the Parisian *cuisine*, and practise the gaieties of life. At Goa, " city of churches," they accommodate themselves to the rule of a Portuguese viceroy, and sell their toys for cowries in the shadows of Cathedral and Inquisition. At Serampore they, until very lately, considered Denmark to be the paramount state, and Copenhagen the metropolis of the world; now indeed, having been recently transferred to British hands, they kiss them with equal reverence. At Hyderabad, nearly the last, if not the last, of the old Mussulman Nizams misgoverns an oppressed people who, if they groan, rebel not. While at Cochin and Travancore, under their own native princes, the Poliars and other castes submit even to be slaves. The Hindoo, if not "gentle," is at least submissive. He is formed by nature and by long habit to be a political Helot. And he is mainly so through the influence of a peculiar institution. What nationality is to others, caste is to the Hindoo. As long as he can preserve inviolate that sacred bond and boundary of his personal, family, social, and religious life he is satisfied. The conditions of his political life are important or unimportant, according to the relations they bear to that charmed circle. So with all other particulars of his environment. All circumstances or happenings are something or nothing, serious or insignificant, in the proportion of their influence on caste. And here we are brought to the characteristic cause of the part which the Hindoos have taken in the Eastern trouble; in no sense was it likely to be, and in no sense has it been, as far as we can see, a national complicity; only has it been a strictly departmental disturbance, a movement along the ranks, by the men who had to bite the greased cartridges, and thus by an act of self-desecration make themselves outcasts alike from society and *swirga*—earth beneath and heaven above. That so small a cause should have produced effects so large and terrible must seem incredible to any inexperienced in Hindoo character. That half a hundred regiments should have revolted in fear of soiling their lips with fat will very likely be taken as a fiction in present and future times. But any person at all familiar with the idiosyncrasies of the race in question will have been prepared by a score of analogous facts, both great and small, to believe even in the cartridge. To recall some two or three of our own experiences:—Not many years ago, a rumour took wind in Madras that the missionaries converted children by sprinkling a white powder over them; rapidly, as if by telegraph, the notion spread itself over the adjacent districts, and in some cases all but emptied, and in many instances decimated, the schools. A collector touched a wafer with his tongue, and immediately his *cutchery* was in rebellion; neither moonshee nor peon would befoul himself with the abominable letter. A lady, giving gratuitous instruction in a girl's school, put her "thimble-finger" to her lips, and straightway the children were withdrawn from the school, in dread of pollution. Not to multiply instances, these we think are sufficient to justify us in believing that the same people who took their children from school in fear of the white powder, who would not touch a letter in fear of a wafer, and who would not let their girls learn sewing in fear of the thimble, would be likely enough to grow disaffected in fear of the greased cartridge, if it were, as it certainly is, equally obnoxious to them; and more especially if their suspicious and superstitious minds had previously been abused by a suggestion of design.

The error in all these cases is to consider the apparent agent apart from that on which it operates. It is not the spark that blasts the rock, but the ignited powder; so it is not the cartridge that caused the mutiny, but the endangered caste. And when the British reader understands that caste is as sacred to a Hindoo as personal liberty or personal nationality is to himself, perhaps he will be able also to understand, in the instance we are considering, the power of an agent otherwise so enormously incongruous and disproportioned to the effect it has assisted to produce. We do not now include in this "result" the horrible cruelties which the fiendish wretches have committed; these are to be traceable to causes, the search for which we deprecate, as it would lead us into caverns foul, dark, and injurious to the moral life. There be some hidden things in the Asiatic nature of which we exclaim with the old Hebrew—"O my soul, come not thou into their secret!"

In looking over the pages of Indian history we find that the present disastrous movement, for which we have ventured to suggest some probable causes, is not without its parallels in character if not in consequence. We have yet space for more than one in this paper,—the mutiny and massacre at Vellore. A little before daybreak on the 10th of July, 1806, the European troops, consisting of four companies of the 64th regiment, were aroused from sleep by a murderous attack upon their barracks by the native soldiery of the garrison. Taken wholly by surprise, and unprepared in every way, they fell by scores beneath the fire of the cowards. Two colonels, thirteen officers, and eighty-two men were killed, and a hundred more were wounded on that fatal morning. A few escaped, one of whom happily found his way to Arcot, about twelve miles off, where the 19th Dragoons were stationed under Colonel Gillespie. Scarcely was the news told when the gallant troops were on their way to the scene of blood; and before ten o'clock on the same morning the 64th were terribly avenged by the death of hundreds of their treacherous assailants. So far the disaster itself—now for the accepted causes, matters of fact and history. Not long before the outbreak, certain general orders had been issued directing sundry changes in the dress of the sepoys : amongst other innovations a turnscrew was to be numbered among the accoutrements, and the ancient turban was to be discarded for a head-dress bearing a resemblance to the shako. The turnscrew, to the ignorant sepoys, assumed the appearance of a cross, the symbol of the Christian religion, and the shako they took to be the hat or *topee*, everywhere in India to this day considered to be the symbol of Western customs; and the whole measure was construed into a crusade against their religious and social prejudices, and more especially against caste ; and so far we have the almost exact antecedent of the cartridge. But the parallel does not stop here. In this town of Vellore, at the very time there lived, as pensioners on the Company's revenue, the sons of Tippoo Sultan, late Mohammedan ruler of the Mysore. Suspicion of connivance at once attached itself to these princes, which subsequent investigation developed into absolute conviction, and they were accordingly sent up to Calcutta for safer custody. And here we have the parallel completed. Moiz-ud-deen the son of Tippoo, and the King of Oude or the Delhi prince, are but duplicates of the same Mohammedan spirit of conspiracy and rebellion, just as the turnscrew-cross and the shako-hat have their part in the cartridge ; nature, national character, tradition, and caste underlying and giving life and force to the whole.

There yet remain, however, about the movement peculiarities which neither Mohammed turbulence nor Hindoo superstition can be found to explain. How is it that disaffection amongst the military should spread so widely and ripen so rapidly, that in a few months or less it should suddenly burst out into a revolt of more than half a hundred regiments? This leads us to glance at certain particulars in the organization and management of the Indian army. That army is composed partly of European regiments and partly of native regiments in proportions that must at once strike the reader as strangely out of proportion. Not having any more recent statistics before us than those of 1853, we quote the following as an approximate estimate:—

Queen's Troops	29,480
Company's European Troops	19,928
Total number of Europeans..........	49,408
Company's Native Troops ...	240,121
Native Contingents	32,000
Total number of Natives............	272,121

Taking these returns as our guide, for every British soldier in India there are six sepoys! The disproportion becomes enormous when it is remembered that the independent and tributary states muster together an army of not less than five hundred thousand native mercenaries; and more enormous still, when the fact is recognized that this army is quartered amongst one hundred and fifty millions of people of kindred blood to the sepoy majority! The wonder is, under such circumstances, that the empire is in existence, not that a mutiny has broken out in this third century of British rule.

The distribution of this army, as a result of its monstrous deformity, is singularly suggestive of insecurity. The European troops, along with some native regiments, are, chiefly, scattered along broken and lengthy frontier lines, partly grouped about suspected districts, the remainder being cut up into "wings" and served out among some score or two of cantonments; leaving vast areas, some of them covered with forts and strong in natural fastnesses, to be occupied wholly by native regiments. And along with this must be coupled the difficulties and dangers attending the transport of European troops, in a country where the shade is almost intolerable, and where cholera and fever are the most faithful of camp followers.

But probably one of the chief elements of danger lies in the make-up and efficiency of the native regiments themselves. The rank and file are wholly natives, the non-commissioned officers are also natives; then follows, as an upper grade, a class of middle-men, all natives, who, with native titles sufficiently imposing, have scarcely the recognized authority or real rank of the most beardless cadet; then at last, like the little head of a show giant perched ridiculously on the summit of a heap of bone and brawn, comes the European officery—a modicum of ensigns, lieutenants, captains, majors, lieut.-colonels, etc. A native regiment on parade is a sight suggestive of a security that has grown into an insanity.—A long line of black faces and "brown besses," broken here and there at long intervals by a solitary pale face and fragile sword! But a native regiment off parade presents yet more serious matter for consideration; drill over and the line broken up, where is the bond of union, the chord of sympathy, that should connect the body with the head? The officers canter off to their bungalows or their mess-room, and the men saunter to their "lines;" each having a distinct and separated life. From the very nature of such a corporation, power and authority are with the "middle men." The pale faces, by their very paleness, their language, habits, religion, and everything else that has gained for them their *status*, are removed from the regiment; they may be fastened on to it like the paste-board head of a pantomime, but the real brain that sends out its nerves through trunk and limb belongs to the black-faced men within—the men who go with the sepoys to their lines, talk with them, worship with them, live like them, and have the same blood running in their veins.

In numerous instances the British officer has striven hard to reach and rule the inner life of his regiment, has bravely set his soul to the work of mastering language and nature, and not always without success. But safety is not in exceptions, however numerous; and, especially in this case, there is no safety that does not as a natural outgrowth result from the whole organization.

Defective as the Indian sepoy regiment is in its very make-up, it becomes so through causes partly inevitable, partly otherwise. The European officers, always too few—at the full scarcely half the number belonging to a Queen's regiment—are in most cases sadly reduced. Owing to climate and other sources of injurious influence, disease sends to the *hill stations*, to the Cape, or homewards, a startling percentage; "private affairs" make sad ravages among the remainder; the staff enforces its demands; while the different departments of a complicated commissariat carry off their prey. These reductions, however, being recognizable as among the contingencies to be expected, we will pass them over with simply calling attention to the fact that, if they are unavoidable, they do not the less on that account weaken the European element in the regiment.

But there is another source of denudation which ought not to be avoidable, and which not only reduces that element numerically, but also deteriorates it in quality. Owing to the exigencies of recent rapid annexation, and the insufficiency and *expensiveness* of the civil service, the Company's military service has been largely drained of its efficient men. Lieutenants and captains have been summoned from their regiments to take upon themselves the duties of commissioners, collectors, and judges; the Company has been sacrificed to the *cutchery*, the sword cast aside for the pen; statutes and tariffs have sent the drill to the route, uniforms have been devoted to the moths, and duty to the dogs. Engineering, surveying, and diplomatic necessities have been allowed to pounce down like so many cannibal ogres on the upper ten; and, at least in one case within our knowledge, the photographic art carried off a victim from the command of his company and attached him as collodionist-general to a foreign commission. We could point to whole provinces where all the European officials, from the first commissioner down to the superintendent of a sheep farm, are men withdrawn from the military service, leaving their vacancies unfilled. Now it is not illogical at least to suppose (due allowance being made for the action of "influence," "interest," etc.) that the men selected for high and responsible posts are generally chosen on account of aptitude and efficiency, thus plainly necessitating a loss to the European element in its highest *desiderata*. Nor is this all. The advantages of these appointments are great—sufficiently so to make them objects of ambition along the whole line. Thus they attract from strictly regimental and general military duties and studies that undivided and devoted attention which alone secures efficiency and success in any profession. Instead of being encouraged to look to his regiment as the sphere of his duty, and the army as the circle of his hopes, the Company's officer is tempted, by a score of posts and places, fat and fair, to do anything but keep his "eyes straight." But there is not to be found in Nagpore, Oude, the Punjab, Pegu, Arracan, the Mysore, and Koory room enough for all the military, and thus some are left to their regiments, many staying by their colours with the willingness of true soldiers doubtlessly; yet many, in the very nature of things, must remain with a feeling of disappointment, and all must have a sense of being left behind to duties from which luckier comrades have gladly escaped, and may be tempted to think that they are bound to a service from which cleverer comrades have been promoted to one of higher claims and consideration. It is not always, under such circumstances, that the marching man can see his honour mirrored in his sword.

That the condition of the Indian army has had its influence on the present disasters must be allowed. The defectiveness of military organization has given some opportunity to disaffection to develop itself into mutiny and revolt. Had the European element in the army been more powerful in quantity, more vitally connected with its inner life, more bound up and identified with its interests, the symptoms of alienation would have been earlier detected, and the disease stopped without the necessity of amputation or the sterner obligation of death.

Nevertheless, the British Empire remains intact. India cannot be lost to England, even by the revolt of seventy thousand sepoys. Already the old heroic regiments of the empire are on their way from their scattered outposts of colonial Britain; ere this also they have heard of it at home; and it will not be long before another Plassey, if the need be, will assert the ancient arms and rule; although no deeds of glory can revivify the dishonoured dead, staunch the wounds of the bereaved, or remove the sense of a national disgrace.

A KAFFIR SHAM-FIGHT.

In 1860, the Duke of Edinburgh—then Prince Alfred, a "middy," not long in his teens—took Natal in his circuit of South Africa. It was, of course, necessary that he should be entertained with something more unusual than a mayor's address, a foundation stone, a triumphal arch, and a ball. In the Cape Colony he had heard Sunday-schools sing, and had shot at springbok. In the Free State he had chased great herds of antelope, gnu, and zebra, over plains as boundless as his own sea. So it was determined that in Natal he should see a mimic Aldershot day *à la* Zulu. The idea was an inspiration, and had descended upon Sir Theophilus Shepstone in a happy moment. At that time Sir Theophilus had not attained to the honours of a K.C.M.G., but he had long been Secretary for Native Affairs to the Natal Government, and knew exactly what his Zulus could do that would be a surprise to the prince. They were perfectly at his command, and he had, as his lieutenant, Goza, whom most of the natives considered their chief. Orders were sent out to the tribes dwelling by the Umgeni, the Umvote, the Tugela, and a score of minor streams, under the far-falling shadow of the Drakenbergen, and amidst the tumbled hills of Inanda, and preparations were speedily made for a splendid display.

The Zulus of Natal are a light-hearted race, fond of quick glancing movement, personal adornment, the music of their own voices, the dance, excitement, and display. It is a pleasure to them to run, to sing as they go, to flourish the club they call the *keerie*, and to hear behind them the rustle of a long string of patches and shreds, like the tail of a kite, which, flying from their girdle as they rush along, catches the wind. For them to be told to get ready for a sham-fight in the presence of the queen's son was joyous news. Not all could go, but the best should—the braves who knew the old style, had the finest equipment, and were skilled to act in concert. Out of the 60,000 able-bodied men of the tribes about 3000 were chosen, and of the women a few scores. Assegais were prohibited as possibly dangerous in the excitement of warlike exercises, and these were left to lie against the walls of the reed-built hut. But shields were taken down and dressed, clubs shaped and tattooed to the fashion, feathers, furs, tails of cow and monkey, skins of leopard, jackal, and deer, were dusted and trimmed, and tigers' teeth and beads were polished and strung together in necklaces and armlets. It was like a taste of old times to the barbarians who, while somewhat tamed by the mild yoke of British rule and accustomed to peace, still remembered the days when war came with almost every year, and the call to arms might come at any cock-crow.

The place chosen for the review was on the south side of the river which sweeps with a swift current by the pretty town of Maritzburg, the capital of Natal. Just there the grass-lands of the mid-country, dotted with thorn-trees, roll in long curves to the river terraces. There are no fences, and the spaces are wide and far-reaching, with low levels for a spectacle, and gentle slopes for spectators. The view around has its own charms. Below, the stream with its border of willows, its broken waters as they whiten over the up-jutting reefs, and its quiet shining surfaces where a deep furrow has been ploughed by the current in the soft earth. Then the town, with its long lines of red roofs, its gardens hedged with rose-bushes, and its open square bordered with young growing trees. Beyond, the great grass hill, with its shadows folded in the hollows. To the right, the valley leading up to the Mission Station where Bishop Colenso learnt criticism from the intelligent Zulu; and, yet more to the right, Tafel Berg, a huge table-mountain, with coronet of rock and robes of green, glowing ever when the sun shines, like a gem. No better spot could have been selected.

The day came—blue above, without a cloud, and clear below, without dust, smoke, or vapour. The citizens of Maritzburg made a little crowd around the prince, who took his stand beneath the Union Jack planted firmly on the hill-side. Below, at some distance, the 3000 Zulus were drawn out in a semi-circular line, which had more the

look of a continuous parti-coloured wall than of an array
of men. A long red streak was followed by a long black
streak, that by a long red-and-white streak, and that by a
long black-and-white streak, each streak being four feet
and a half high, and all the streaks being surmounted by a
long dark band. This singular appearance was caused by
the regimental shields, which, formed of ox-hides of varying
colours, reached from the foot nearly to the chin, and were
held by the men, closely dressed, so as to overlap each
other. There was thus presented a wall of leather, and
as the hairy sides of the hides were to the front, and the
companies were arranged according to the colour of the
hair, the wall seemed painted in different hues. The long
black band or common coping surmounting the wall was
formed of the 3000 Zulu heads. The effect at a distance
was peculiar, but monotonous. A British regiment, standing at ease at a distance of a few hundred yards, wearies
even the patriotic eye with a sense of overmuch oneness;
but the British soldier keeps his elbows free, and the back
light glimmers through his legs. Not so with the Zulus.
All that could be seen was leather—nothing but leather,
excepting the black streak along the top. Unquestionably
the idea of solidity was conveyed. The line was a fortification, and looked impenetrable. As the formation was
kept up for some time, the quality of steadiness was also
suggested. Another suggestion was that of mystery.
What was there behind that motionless, creviceless wall?
Curiosity was sharpened by the singular sounds which the
half-moon of leather sent forth, now from one horn, then

the other, anon from the centre, and now from the whole line. It was as the play of thunder with its echoes, at times sudden and startling, hoarse and threatening, and again muttering, low and distant. Regiment cried to regiment, and chorus followed solo, as passion beat time in the 3000 hearts behind the leather. The general result was that of brooding sullenness, flashing now and then into eager anger and sharp desire for action—a fit prelude to the shoutings, groans, and shrieks of a real battle-field. What the actual words of the chant were I cannot say, but have no doubt that they were most bloodthirsty. Desire, akin to that which leads a traveller to the rim of Vesuvius when it is beginning to bellow, induced me to approach the mysterious line.

Nearness certainly gave new terrors to the eye. The shields remained as they had been at a distance—all leather, and no prunella—but the dark band above resolved itself into a hideous row of heads, half hidden behind a fringe of hair-tufts. "Eyes straight" is no part of the Zulu drill, and the whole line was terrible "with fine frenzy rolling," while sharp fangs glittered from mouths chanting curses. A flank movement, successfully executed with the dash of a special correspondent, enabled me to take the 3000 in the rear, and then I saw what I saw. I need not attempt the impossible task of describing the *tout ensemble*, but will pick out one of the rumbling braves, and turn him round to the view. I select this huge fellow with a cock's feather sticking out from between his front teeth, and take him from the ranks. His head-dress is a coronet of dusky ostrich-feathers towering to the height of a guardsman's bearskin; the plumes are fastened together by the quills only, so that they rustle freely at every movement of the body. Immediately beneath, circling the brow, is a roll of tiger-skin, from which descends over eye, ear, and mouth, almost to the shoulder, a fringe of long coarse hair, half hiding, half disclosing, fierce glances and the gnashing of teeth. A similar, but smaller, fringe of grizzly bristles is fastened over the upper lip. So much for head and face, plume, and mask. From his neck and shoulders downwards to his knees, his body is covered with the tails of monkeys and tigers, and strips of various hides, strung together in girdles. His waist is girt about with tufts of lion's mane and cow-hair; so are his arms above and below the elbow, and at the wrist. Circlets of some brute's hair are about his knees, and anklets of the same material finish his grim uniform. Within all this load of horrors is a lithe, muscular, sinewy, black, and well-greased body, and within that are the passions of a savage. His shield is as hard as wood, and tough with good dressing. It is shaped into an oval, fastened to an upright of lance-wood, which is the handle, and pieced and stitched with patient skill. This he carries in his left hand, together with three or four assegai sticks without the heads, while in his right hand he grasps a club well knobbed.

This is one of the 3000; the others are like unto him; and no beast prowling in jungle, or lurking in cave, by day or night, is half so horrible. By a piece of good fortune, I caught the great chief, Goza, at his toilette. I had seen him many a time in *mufti*, and was familiar with his white hat, crape band, and thick pilot coat, with big gaping pockets. At this heroic moment, however, Goza is the high-stepping leader and great captain, preparing for the field. His warriors are around him; his nostrils quiver and his eyes flash. Goza has no white and well-craped hat now, no pilot coat, no decent pantaloons. The humdrum garments of civilization are discarded, and he is, with the help of a dozen squires and pages, putting himself into a complicated garniture of feathers, hair fringes, tufts, tails, tusks, teeth, and skins, which few menageries or zoological gardens could furnish.

Goza struts, shakes his terrors, snorts like a war-horse, rolls his eyes, casts out far-reaching glances of command, brandishes his sword, and moves to the front of his army in great leaps and bounds, as though each movement were a conquest. Goza has his captains, who are all dressed in humble imitation of his finery, just as the 3000 are like the private we took just now the liberty of inspecting.

After the prince had ridden through the ranks, the evolutions began. Goza gave the sign, and one of the regiments marched rapidly, with a leaping movement, towards the spectators, sending forth at the same time a hurricane of shrieks and yells. Surging up to the very feet of the prince, they retreated, still keeping their faces towards him; they advanced again, sprung aloft with great brute-like bounds, knelt, couched, hid themselves behind their shields, lay still as death, darted upwards into the air with startlingly sudden noise, brandished their spearsticks, and drummed their shields with knee and foot. At last the time came for sighting the enemy, and the charge. Goza gave a sign which was equivalent to " Up, guards, and at 'em !" and away they went, still in line, but in passionate pulses of movement rather than in a march, raging, giving mouth, eager as panthers for blood. At another sign, the charge became a retreat. In almost perfect order the line changed face, the shields were swung round to the back, and a compact wall of hard-bound hide was presented to the pursuing foe.

As the men fled, they changed their cries to serpent-like hisses, as if to warn those who chased them that they were deadly if too closely pressed upon. Each regiment in its turn displayed its ability to be terrible. Then all united in a more complicated performance. The different bands charged each other, coiled themselves up in folds, slid through each other's ranks, undid the tangle, and rushed into line, each man quivering as with suppressed passion, the whole 3000 feeling as one. There they stood for a moment, eager, leaning forward as if held only by a leash. In an instant the leash was slipped, and, with redoubled yells, the regiments became a frantic mob, each man hurling himself forwards and upwards with a fury that seemed to turn each feather and hair into instruments of war. The braves were fiends ; the passion was madness.

Goza seemed to comprehend that the line of danger had been reached. At all events, he flew at some two or three of the most frantic and forward, and struck their shields with his sword, making the leather chips fly into the air. Probably it was all acting; if so, it was brilliantly clever. The last scene was as singular as any. After two hours of hard sham-fighting, and when the regiments had formed for the march off, and were chanting in low monotone, about a hundred women, clad only in a very scanty girdle of beads, came running, with prying looks and bent forms, into the field. They were cruel in their aspect, and armed with short large-headed clubs. Every now and then they stooped, and aimed heavy blows, and as they did so they screamed with triumph. Their task was to kill the wounded.

It was evening before the spectacle was over, and I left late. As I passed along the lower terraces of the river-slope I was overtaken by a regiment, at the quick march, hastening to the camping fires. The men moaned and wailed as they went, and had a look of hunger in their eyes, as well as of excitement. By-and-by the fires came in view, with dark, fantastic, monstrous forms flitting about them in the smoke, great hunks of roasting flesh, and cauldrons of steaming maize-porridge. Here and there were groups of ravenous eaters, gnawing half-raw morsels of beef, and gulping down huge ladle-loads of scalding brose. The bivouac was as savage as the review. The revelry lasted far into the night; but by the morning the army had departed, leaving behind only the bones of many an ox.

REVERENCE, AND THE WANT OF IT IN THIS COLONY.

Written at Grahamstown, 1869.

> "Let knowledge grow from more to more,
> But more of reverence in us dwell;
> That mind and soul, according well,
> May make one music as before,
> But vaster——"

WHEN Wilhelm Meister entered the "great institution" where he desired to place his son Felix, his attention was arrested by the singular gestures of the children. "The youngest laid their arms crosswise over their breasts, and looked cheerfully to the sky; those of middle size held their hands on their backs, and looked smiling on the ground; the eldest stood with a frank and spirited air, their hands stretched down; they turned their heads to the right, and formed themselves into a line,—whereas the others kept separate, each where he chanced to be." The Three, when asked by Meister for an explanation of these postures, said: " Well-formed, healthy children bring much into the world. One thing, at least, Nature does not give them, and yet it is on this one thing that all depends for making man in every point a man. If you can discover it yourself, speak out." Wilhelm was silent. Then the Three, after a suitable pause, exclaimed, " Reverence!" Wilhelm hesitated. " Reverence!" cried they a second time. " All want it; perhaps you yourself." The three gestures, Wilhelm is further informed, are the expressions of a threefold reverence,—reverence for what is above us, reverence for what is under us, reverence for that which is level with us. After some further explanation, Wilhelm exclaimed, " I see a glimpse of it."

It would be a happy thing for this colony if the system of the Three could, in this respect, be introduced into all its educational institutions, whether the family, school, or college. If any man will observe, and reflect on what he observes, he will also have "a glimpse" of the value of reverence to character, and the all but utter absence of it in children. It is commonly remarked of the young people of all new countries, that they spring up suddenly into men and women, hurrying over the stage of boyhood and girlhood. To whatever other auxiliary causes this is to be attributed, it is to be traced, in a great measure, to a lack of the repressive retarding, slowly maturing influence of reverence. The youth of new countries are eminently " fast." This is a modern word, which the modern life of old countries has added to our vocabulary. But the rapid running up into premature flower and seed is a more marked phenomenon of new communities than of old;

because in the youth of freshly planted societies is to be seen the abrupt development of the whole man-germ into manhood, which is too frequently nothing else but man-mockery. In Europe some young men live riotously. Here, almost all children come of age at a leap. And this is largely owing to the absence of the salutary pressure of reverence upon the mind and soul, as much as to anything else. Indeed, many of the other apparent causes of this prematurity would, if rightly examined, resolve itself into this one. The freedom of life, the feebleness of the cohesive power in society, the conditions favourable to individual development, rudeness of circumstance, the want of all that evidence of the genius and labour, the worth and dignity of man which an ancient civilization has accumulated, the presence of rough, uncultured nature, and of rude, savage, and simple but degraded man,—all these characteristics of new countries are but so many reasons why there is so little reverence in their young people. The charm and usefulness of a long spring-time are wanting, because this retarding force is absent. There is so little reverence, because there is so little in the conditions of life to excite it—so much less than in those old lands where authority, order, achievement, example, widening precedent, a long-inherited sentiment, and the mighty works of successive generations unite to throw a shadow on the young mind, in which it slowly grows, and mellows as it ripens.

This absence of circumstances favourable to the dawn of reverence imposes a responsibility upon education.

The fanciful symbolism of the Three, which, in some respects, looks like a school edition of Ritualism, may suggest nothing for imitation; but the idea of teaching reverence by a well-considered machinery of means is worthy of grave attention. What this machinery is to be is a difficult question. The professor who would propound a solution, based upon a comprehension of the nature of children, and of the importance of reverence as a human affection, whether natural or induced, would deserve the name and reputation of the founder of the educational system best suited to a colony. It is possible that the centralization of our higher schools, the substitution of one or two great institutions for the present many small ones, would be friendly to the natural growth of circumstances favourable to the planting and nursing of a reverent temper. If any institution similar, as to its organization and equipment, to a great public school in England could by united effort be reproduced here, part of the desirable work would be provided for. A building of some pretence to magnificence, offices of dignity, a staff of earnest, scholarly, masterful gentlemen, a rigid but humane discipline, badges of distinction, and, above all, a college chapel, bright, vivacious, inspiriting liturgical service, and a priest with eyes and voice like Arnold's, would work a revolution in the spirit of boys trained under such influences. The sense of size, labour, and skill in human work,—the consciousness of a rule for life other than individual wilfulness, of the claims of others, of the obligations of religion,—would have a chance of a beginning amidst such surroundings. At present, division and littleness deprive our schools of dignity. There is nothing in the plain, scanty building, the mean endowments, the meagre staff, and the surface discipline of our score of colleges and thousand and one academies, seminaries, gymnasiums, and establishments to counteract the unimpressive circumstances of general colonial life. To give magnitude and fulness to our educational institutions by centralization would, however, do but little more than favour reverence when its seed had been sown. The planting and direct culture would still have to be provided for; and it would be necessary for educators to consider by what means that which the Three declared to be not natural could best be implanted. Ceremony, secrecy, mystic symbolism, are not likely to form part of a school course in these days. But there never was a time when there was a firmer belief in the power of educational system to form the character and to remedy natural defect. The one case of Laura Bridgman shows to what a marvellous extent the first perception and the first consciousness—apparently the very elements of mind and soul—may be created, or summoned into life and light out of a blank and blind chaos. There is every reason to suppose that, if the conditions of education were improved by massing our institutions, the machinery of education would be improved also, and that more subtle, searching, and comprehensive influences would be brought into play. So that if the importance of reverence to individual and national character were recognized by professors, there would be the discovery and the use of the discipline necessary to excite and nurture it. Less of dividedness and more of centralization, less of smallness and more of breadth, less of poverty and more of pomp and circumstance, would favour perfection in the science and art of education, and all together would tend to the growth of reverential habit, as well as of all other excellences.

It is pretty certain that if reverence be not grafted on the youth of a colony, adult life will, as a rule, be without it. A system of discipline, and a set of artificial circumstances, may be invented for the boy and be applied to his senses and to all his faculties, with a view to a particular result. But for the man there is no artificial system of discipline; outside life is everything to him. And in a new country a modern settlement, what is it? Everything is rude, elemental, unimpressive. Nor is it that colonial circumstance is marked by simplicity. There is a bareness which is not simplicity. There is nothing beautiful or dignified in simplicity which is not the result of combination, harmony, and great labour to hide complexity of parts in unity of result. There is more of that true simplicity which finds its way into the mind, and fills it with awe, in the jointed and piled masonry of the pyramids than in the huddled cairn, much more in the dome of St. Peter's or St. Paul's than in the rude cupola of a Kaffir's hut, much more in the beautiful statue which consumed a lifetime in its perfecting than in the log which a savage hews and hacks into shape with a few blows. Similarly, there is more of that simplicity which imparts dignity to individual and social character in the conditions of an ancient and still enduring civilization than in the phase of a modern settlement. There is, indeed, no simplicity without much art, no simplicity without much culture. Paris or London has more simplicity in its circumstance, its life, its manners, than has New York. The absence of number or of quantity is not essential to simplicity; yet no error is more common than this; and in no respect more so than in relation to the conditions of human life. An old-world man fancies that he will find simplicity in the new world. The man of the town believes enthusiastically in the simplicity of the village. The villager sees in the solitariness of the farm a simplicity still severer than his own. And it is too generally supposed that this simplicity of circumstance, which is all but wholly fictitious, is conducive to simplicity of character—a conclusion which is as erroneous as the premises from which it is drawn. It is a mistake to think that because the fittings and furniture of colonial life are bare and scant, they are favourable to the severer and graver virtues, and, above all, of reverence. And it is the recognition of this which makes it all the more necessary that the development of this great quality of a manly character should be one of the tasks of education. The habit once formed under the influence of a wise artifice would, in whatever circumstance, find the means of its growth. The youth trained by an adjusted discipline to regard all outward things, whether above, beneath, or on his level, as having claims upon him not to be disregarded, would, on passing from a school or college into the unimpressive life of a colony, discover on all sides objects to revere.

If the colonist of the day, untrained by education, be observed in his relations to the various departments of life, it will be seen how defective he is in this feeling of reverence, and how unfavourable to its development are his surroundings. It may be said that the unfriendliness of his circumstances may be taken not only to account for his deficiency in this respect, but also to excuse or justify it. Or it may be pleaded that if there be little or nothing to excite reverence, there is no need for it. But with this, as with all other virtues, the absence of that which favours it is in itself a reason for its culture. It is one of the fruitful errors of a newly settled people to think that character is at liberty to conform itself to circumstance; to be rude and selfish because nature and conditions are rude, and because society gives way to self. If the general experience of civilized man has proved any possible human feeling to be in itself good, it ought to be developed and nurtured, let the outer life be what it may. It is no longer thought that the history of the Jews is too sacred to be used like any other history, for purposes of illustration, and the Decalogue may, therefore, be referred to as showing how supremely important the great Lawgiver held it to be to cultivate reverence in his followers at a time when they were about to become colonists, and enter on a new national life amidst circumstances especially hostile to it. All of the ten commandments ordain reverence—reverence for that which was above, under, and level to the emigrant

Jews—reverence for the objects and means of religion, for the family, for life, for property, for personal and relative rights. This obligation was laid upon the minds and hearts of the people by elaborate ceremony, impressed by lofty mysteries, and enforced by penalty, when they were about to pass slowly through a wilderness to a country only to be possessed and settled at the cost of many wars. This is but an illustration as it is here employed, and nothing more. But it suggests, if it does not help to prove, that the absence of circumstances favourable to reverence is not to be taken as a reason why it should be neglected as if it were unnecessary. In referring to the unimpressiveness of the conditions of life, we do but give one of the chief arguments for the intentional and systematic cultivation of a virtue so much disregarded in this as in other colonies.

As Wilhelm Meister passed through the district which lay about the institution he sought, "he noticed, with new surprise, that the further they advanced, a vocal melody more and more sounded towards him from the fields. Whatever the boys might be engaged with, whatever labour they were carrying on, they accompanied it with singing." Longfellow is not an authority equal to Goethe, but he has pretty much the same idea in "The Building of the Ship:"

> "Build me straight, O worthy master!
> Staunch and strong, a goodly vessel.
> * * * * *
> The merchant's word,
> Delighted, the master heard;
> For his heart was in his work, and the heart
> Giveth grace unto every art."

The idea in both these passages is, that there is that in

all labour, whether of the field or the workshop, which may have a cheerful reverence paid to it. There is at the present day a custom in India which expresses the very same opinion in a way which is thoroughly Oriental, and therefore extravagant. On a certain day in the year each man, by the force of an Eastern imagination, and with the freedom of an Eastern piety, turns the implement which is the symbol of his craft, and the chief means of his support, into a minor deity, and worships it with the sacrifice of flowers and with ablutions. The learned man takes his book, the clerk his pen, the soldier his sword, the smith his hammer, the weaver his shuttle, the field-labourer his plough, and going with gay solemnity to the water-side, each instrument, decorated with garlands and sanctified with water, becomes transfigured, sacred, divine, worthy of worship. This is an oriental and pagan way of saying that a joyous reverence may well be given to the occupations which are so necessary to life and by which so much of lifetime is consumed. The disciples of the Three sang hymns as they toiled, the ship-builder gave his heart to his work, and the pagan Hindoo worshipped the symbol of his craft,—all illustrating, as we say, the truth that reverence is due to labour. But the best evidence that such duty is rendered is the evidence of good works.

The song of the digger is nothing unless it giveth rhythm and earnest force to the stroke of the spade; the heart of the ship-master may as well be elsewhere unless it giveth grace unto the art; so, also, the pagan's worship is worthless as it is extravagant unless the worshipped tool is used with a tender touch and an honest purpose. Good work shows reverence for work, and a just appreciation of the great place work has in the economy and discipline of life.

In this colony work is notoriously bad. It is bad because it is not highly considered; and, being bad, it excites no respect. Of late improvement may have dawned, but as yet the light of intelligence has to struggle with the dense darkness in the midst of which our ignorant industries have been groping. There is scarcely a department of production that hitherto has not brought the colony into disrepute. The gifts of nature and the acquisitions of tardy enterprise are treated with a rude, slovenly, blind hand, spoiling everything it touches. This is not the place for a description of the almost brutal methods of culture and manufacture which have been, and still are, too much in vogue amongst us. To do so would be to repeat a tale told a hundred times in the newspapers, and reiterated to weariness at agricultural dinners. It would, however, be unpardonable to pass by the sad proof of a want of that thoughtfulness, that sensitive regard to the relations of all acts, which is the very substance of reverence, thrust upon the public by the late calamitous fires. To burn the grass is one of the labours of our agriculture which may be necessary. If so, it not the less on that account involves, or ought to involve, great responsibility. And yet on a day of intense heat and much wind, at a time when herb and tree are like tinder, and in the neighbourhood of great forests and prosperous homesteads, the brand is flung about as if the work, which a man might well begin upon his knees in fear and trembling, were mere heedless sport. The vast, unfenced, sparsely occupied, poorly fertilized lands of a new country tempt the husbandman to a savage agriculture which has little or no regard for beauty in nature, or right in property, or sacredness in life.

It can scarcely be doubted that the transfer of the rougher work of the colony to the natives is a reason why labour of that kind is treated by the dominant race with slight respect. This has always been the case in countries in which any special tasks have been imposed on a subject people, whether slaves, captives, helots, villeins, pariahs, coolies, or conquered savages. The occupations of these despised people fall into contempt, and make it shameful to engage in them. All history, whether ancient or modern, teems with examples of this. In the present day, the Southern States of America afford a striking illustration of the rapidity with which a race accustomed to hold industry and honest toil in good repute can have its ancestral habits wholly changed by the presence of an abject people, on whom the hard work of the country is imposed. When, under the Austrian kings of Spain, most of the mechanical crafts and the various branches of commerce fell into the hands of foreign immigrants, the Spaniard, although not long before celebrated for his skill in some manufactures, thought it a disgrace to soil his fingers with Segovian cloths or take interest for his wasting capital. In India there is no Brahmin but would deem himself to have lost caste were he to carve the sacred image to which he is ready to bow down and worship as his god. This degradation of labour by its association with a degraded class is inevitable, and is to be modified only by a removal, as far as possible, of artificial difference between classes. The abolition of slavery in America will have a direct influence on the consideration in which all manner of work is held there. The labourer being no longer a slave, his labour is not slavish. In this colony slavery has long been abolished, and that source of danger to the dignity of work is removed. But our labouring class is still savage, ignorant, barbarous, and heathen, and as long as this is the case labour will be debased in the eyes of the colonist. This has its remedy in a properly adapted education. There are some who think that education spoils the native for labour. This, in some cases, arises from possibly wrong systems of training in which natives have been taught, or it arises from narrow views. At all events, it is certainly true that brutal, untaught, wild men spoil the colonist for labour. The tendency of this is unquestionably towards irreverence for work. This effect in its present stage of growth may not be apparent to the unobservant eye, but it exists and will display itself more and more unless the remedies are applied. We can pursue this subject no further; but it may be said that the power of association to affect the estimate in which anything is held is nowhere more strikingly to be seen than in the department of human labour. Let any work, no matter how difficult and beautiful in itself, be assigned to a despised class, and it becomes despicable. Let any work, no matter how coarse, become the monopoly of a privileged class, as is the case with the farrier's craft amongst some Mussulmans, and it becomes dignified. Modifying the thought somewhat, but not essentially, it is found that the association of work with loftiness of character, the unloosing of a slave's latchet, will transcend the sense of worth; while the consciousness of "the great Taskmaster's eye" will give a living meaning to George Herbert's verse :—

> " A servant with this clause
> Makes drudgery divine ;
> Who sweeps a room as for Thy laws,
> Makes that and the action fine."

To charge the colony with a want of reverence for the fine arts would be preposterous. There can be no regard for that which can scarcely be said to have an existence. Perhaps music may be held to be an exception. We believe the ability to appreciate the great masters, skill in execution, and even talent for original composition, are present in the colony; while no *artiste* of any merit visits the Cape and is not understood. Of late, creditable attempts have been made in more towns than one to pay careful and practical homage to the masterpieces of Handel and Mendelssohn. There are few villages that have not some musical organization. We have been assured by the managers of professional companies that in some of the obscurer towns, partly inhabited by foreigners, there is evidence of much musical culture. Most undoubtedly there is no country in which there are more pianos. There is a Broadwood, a Collard, or an

Allison in almost every house, and in well-nigh every farm. At the hours of morning practice, which extend from sunrise to noon, there is no open window through which a torrent of melody does not rush, and the air is more than tremulous with the vibrations of twice ten thousand keys. In whatsoever house there is no piano, there is an accordion, while on the frontier there is not a Kaffir who has not a Jew's harp. In the Eastern garrison towns, so enthusiastic is the reverence paid by the natives to martial music, that a crowd of dancers attend the regimental bands along the whole line of the Sunday march to church. To give some account of the state of musical culture in the colony would be worth the while of some one well versed in the subject.

It would be wrong to say that the colony has had no painters. On the other hand, it would be wrong to say that the colony has greatly valued those it has had. Bowler is seeking fortune at Mauritius. I'ons is making no fortune at Grahamstown. Nor can it be said that these artists have had no recommendation from merit. I'ons has succeeded wonderfully in expressing the fulness and freshness of savage life in the face of the Kaffir, and his work, if proper respect be paid to it, will preserve the faithful portraiture of races which in the course of time will be found in history and picture alone. The water-colour landscapes and the marine sketches of Bowler are, for the most part, faithful copies of some of the finest scenery our coast, river, and mountain can give. His "Wolf River by Moonlight" is worthy reverent admiration for the artistic truthfulness and sympathy with which it represents a beautiful scene beautifully, so that any common eye might see its meaning. The colony has also some amateurs whom it might well value, but whose names would have but little signification were we to mention them, as their works are but little known. There are not wanting those who can love and understand this art, and by some means or other a few good paintings have found their way to the colony, and are understood. Cape Town, by levying contributions or private collections, is able to form a respectable art exhibition, from which great names are not wholly absent. And there are those who can write a fair criticism, discriminating faults from beauties, and thus help to the growth of an intelligent taste. It must not be forgotten, also, that there has been at least one attempt to establish a school of art; and it would be irreverent on our part to overlook the fact that we have photographic artists who are really worthy of that name, if the study of the laws of their craft and a determination to master its agencies, with a view to truth and taste in the expression of life as well as form, entitle them to the distinction. Still, for all this, and notwithstanding that photographs abound in the colony more plentifully than even pianos, it would be an exaggeration to say that art is present; and such being the case, it would be unreasonable to complain that a reverence for it is absent. The time may come when more of our youth may be able to visit the renowned galleries and studios of Europe, and bring back with them, if not inspiration, yet the memory of a great glory and a dissatisfying sense of the bareness of colonial life. This regretful recollection and this consciousness of want may, when wealth—possessed by more hands, accumulated in larger sums, and placed at the disposal of more cultured and liberal minds—has the power to obey desire, lead to the exchange of our gold for some of the precious products of the old-world art genius; and thus the knowledge of what is meant by a picture and by painting may dawn upon the colony, and the love of them may even suggest endeavour. With skies and an atmosphere like ours, mountains that hold both light and shade in charmed masses upon their sides, plains enamelled with fair flowers, bays curved as the line of beauty and flooded with bright water, long lines of tumbling surf, and an ocean on either side, it cannot be said that Nature is niggard of her lessons. All that is wanted is the intervention of the teacher, to show how the lesson is to be learnt. A broad, truthful work from a great hand would do this most effectually.

Of sculpture the colony possesses fewer specimens than of painting. Sir George Grey is our only statue. There is an obelisk at Port Elizabeth. A fountain stands hard by the Cathedral of St. George's at Grahamstown. The massive pulpit of the Dutch Reformed Church at Cape Town is guarded by two huge lions carved in wood, and that of the Lutheran Church rests on the brawny shoulders of two giants in mahogany. The catalogue is scanty. The influence of the works themselves is not great. Reverence seeks the shade, but is not cherished by theirs. The lions and the giants, being where they are, may, by the confusions which are sometimes occasioned by association, be perchance mistaken for objects of public worship. No such accident invests either the statue, the obelisk, or the fountain with any chance of respect, and in themselves these works, though rare, are not wonderful. The colony knows less of sculpture than of painting. And yet, unless savage life should speedily cease to be savage, and clothe itself in the squalid rags of civilization, there are few countries where the human figure could be studied to more advantage than here. The Kaffir, like the ancient Greek, presents, not in the studio only, but in the freedom of everyday life, models of fineness in form and grace in action, while his kaross or blanket falls in rounded, sweeping lines from the shoulder. It would be worth the while of our modern sculptors to take Kaffirland, as well as Rome, within their tours. Were the chisel once at work here in the hands of a genius, this art would, if second-hand clothes were prohibited on the east of the Kei, have rare chances of flourishing and making itself respected.

The great modern art critic says, "There are only two fine arts possible to the human race, sculpture and painting. What we call architecture is only the association of these in noble masses, or the placing them in fit places. All architecture other than this is mere *building*." In another of his works he says that the function of architecture is, as far as may be, to tell us about that Nature which lies remote from towns, "to possess us with memories of her quietness; to be solemn and full of tenderness, like her, and rich in portraitures of her; full of delicate imagery of the flowers we can no more gather, and of the living creatures now far away from us in their own solitude." If this be architecture, and these be its functions, there are few kinds of human work more worthy of reverence; but at the same time it must be confessed that the colony has yet to possess it, and therefore knows nothing of its influences. We have "mere *building*," but no architecture. Architects there are who are doing honest work with such opportunity and material as they have; but their scope is narrow, and their successes are few. Perhaps the only notable thing in this dual art in the colony is the ceiling of the great Dutch Church at Cape Town. The space is vast; and in a huge crowded city of narrow streets and extended masses of masonry, it would do what Ruskin says architecture should do,—it would be a symbol of the over-arch and spread of the sky, of which the narrow, interminable streets and the smoky atmosphere of big towns allow but scanty glimpses. Cape Town streets are not very wide, but the town itself is small, and a few minutes' walk from its most crowded part brings the whole heavens to view. As a substitute for Nature, therefore, the ceiling is not wanted; and if the truth be told, the architect himself, who lived long before Ruskin began to explain the meaning and use of art, had no thought of imitating the span of the firmament. He aimed at a human work of great magnitude when compared with other human works of the kind, and he hoped to succeed in striking the imagination and producing a feeling of reverence suitable to the uses of the place. The appearance of this building from without is mean and unimpressive, and no injury is done to any æsthetic interest by hiding a bald side from view by a row of modern offices. It is possible, however, that the designer thought that it would be a useless expenditure of skill and means to attempt any display of exterior grandeur on a site with such a background as Table Mountain. Even St. Paul's would look poor and dwarfed beneath that mighty work of Nature's masonry, about whose base all Cape Town lies like a huddled landslip, the mere crumbling of a buttress. The architect of the Dutch Reformed Church, with its wide, pillarless ceiling, understood, after all, where to put forth his art with the best chance of getting men to honour it. And in this he suggests the lesson that if art is to be reverenced, it may endeavour to represent Nature when she is absent, but must not compete with her while she is present.

It would be unjust to say that there is but little reverence in the colony for law. It may, indeed, be questioned whether there is any free people amongst whom the authority of law is more regarded; although it has been declared by some, who have a right to speak on such a subject, that the principles of equity, truthfulness, and honesty, on which all righteous law is founded, are not held in equal respect. Let this be as it may, it is undoubtedly the case that, although the executive arm is comparatively feeble, the decisions of law are never resisted, and notwithstanding the extraordinary facilities of escape, they are resorted to but seldom. There is no lawlessness, except amongst the natives in the remote outskirts of society. A magistrate with a policeman or two will preserve order in border districts a thousand miles from the seat of Government. That is to say, the people of those distant places will respect order and authority in the mere office of the magistrate. This is a testimony which, if it be true, proves an excellence of no mean class.

Patriotism may be said to be the highest form of reverence for the State; and as yet there is but little of it in this colony. One possible reason of this is the fact that the Cape is a colony, a dependency on a distant country, with no distinctly separate national life. In recognizing this we are not advancing it as a motive for desiring independence. The advantages of our present connection with Great Britain outweigh the disadvantages, whatever they may be. Disentangling it from any question of this kind, the influence of the fact referred to on the public regard for the State is worth a passing note. Is it not the case that there is a stronger sense of the claims of all that is meant by the phrase " my country " in the Orange Free State than in either of the British South African colonies? That there are some annexationists does but bring out into bolder relief the stubborn patriotism of the majority.

Another cause of the feebleness of the national feeling is the dividedness of the population. It will necessarily take time to weld together the peoples and tongues of British South Africa, so as to make them owe and beget a reverent love of the State—the form of society which includes and unites all classes, institutions, interests, and individuals. A third cause may be sought for in the fact that a British colony is a democracy. All democracies, in some important respects, favour the development of personal interests or selfishness. The individualizing forces are stronger than the uniting forces. In a colony of large area and scanty population, this tendency becomes more pronounced. In such a case the action towards union, when there is any, and the attachments and passions attending it, stop short, for the most part, at "localism," a term which is well understood in this colony. And if there is but little reverence for the State, neither is there much for such political institutions as we have. Whether a reform in the development theory would have the effect of increasing or diminishing the public respect for Government is a moot question, which it would be out of place to discuss here. It may, however, be said that no greater misfortune can happen to a country than for its people to hold political office and function in contempt.

Passing on to another topic, would it be wrong to consider a reverence for all life, and especially for human life, to be an essential part of modern civilization? We say modern civilization, because it is a notorious fact of history that some of the most cultured and, in some respects, most fastidious peoples of antiquity were coldly or cruelly indifferent to suffering, utterly reckless of the lives of others, and ignorant of the passion of humanity. In modern times, and in the foremost countries, law as well as custom has taken the dumb beast under its protection, while the growing reverence for human life has been shown in the abolition of coarse and dangerous sports, the repression of duelling, the prohibition of trades like that of the chimney sweep, the restrictions on the employment of children in factories, the multiplication of hospitals, the better regulation of asylums, the less frequent resort to corporal punishment in both army and navy, the purging of our criminal law of its once shameful rigours, the privacy with which capital executions are invested, and the increasing influence of justice, and desire for peace in the councils of nations. This high regard for the great and precious principles and fact of life in all creatures is one of the glories of the time, and it may well awaken anxiety in any people if they have reason to think that they have about them conditions unfavourable to this excellence. As long as slavery existed in the United States, and as long as certain laws relating to the treatment of slaves and narrowing their rights prevailed, there were in that great country circumstances which, while they lasted, hardened the heart of the South, and which, had they not been removed, would at this moment be weakening the bonds of sympathy between man and man, and turning the wide consciousness of humanity into the petty but fierce pride of a privileged class. It is, indeed, a mistake to suppose that the want of reverence for the body and life of a slave has no influence on that feeling in reference to men not slaves. Familiarity with any form of cruelty to any creature in time does its work on the whole nature, and influences the individual in all his relations. But it is not our duty to consider other countries.

It will, however, be readily understood why we have referred to America, instead of at once examining conditions in South Africa. There is something in the circumstances occasioned by the presence of the African races here which may be said to be analogous to the circumstances occasioned by slavery in the Southern States. The word "nigger" condenses and includes nearly all that we wish to suggest. An inferior, naturally separated, savage race, by what it is and by what it is not, by what it does and by what it omits, tempts the colonists to a contempt for life which, let it be as degraded as it may, is still human. This is seen most markedly in the outskirts of our settlements. It is notorious that in the distant borders of the outlying states, where law is weak and treaties are of no avail, to shoot a black man is little less than a piece of sport. Killing is no murder in such a case. Nearer to the heart of authority, custom and opinion are more under restraint; but it is not too much to say, that throughout the whole of South Africa the reverence for human life is endangered by the contact of colonists with natives. Kaffir wars, Basuto pillages, Koranna inraids, and the thievish habits of these people, increase the aversion and give bitterness to the contempt with which the white man regards the black, and make him less regardful of the act of taking life. It must in justice be said that it is not often that the settlers in the older colonies are publicly known to commit cruelties on the natives, or wantonly to inflict death; nor can one be charged with any inequality whatsoever in matters relating to the person or to life. But while this is gladly allowed, it would be wrong, most injurious to national manners, to overlook the probable influence of conditions which prevail in the South African colonies more than in any other dependency of the British Crown. The reasons for a humane policy towards the native races are to be sought not only in the records of the Aborigines Protection Society, but also in the lessons of history and in the immutable laws on which all true excellence, whether of personal or national character, is founded.

In considering a subject of this nature there is a danger of overstepping reasonable limits, and forcing an idea into departments of life to which it may have no special relation. It may be that a want of reverence for religion is not one of the peculiar faults of this colony. This is a question which may be left undecided by us. It may, however, be as well to glance at one or two things which may be presumed to be unfavourable to the exercise of reverence. Were it possible, as we think it is, to distinguish between a reverence for religion and the religious sentiment itself, it would not be difficult to show that the absence of a State church here, as in other British colonies, has the tendency to lessen the respect for religion viewed as a part of national manners. A State church is clothed with authority and is rich in accessories. It has the means of adorning itself with learning and of arming itself with social power. Accumulating wealth from the public estate and private benevolence, it presents itself everywhere to the eye in the grandeur of its temples and the pomp and power of its chief priests, while its lofty and assured position sheds a certain dignity upon the meanest of its fanes and the humblest of its ministers. All this has its influence, not only upon those who are themselves the adherents of this favoured church, but also on the whole circle of society, including those who do not conform as well as those who do. There can be but little doubt that the decent regard which in England is paid to the tabernacle is the offspring of the respect which has been commanded for centuries by the massive and long-enduring glories of the cathedral. Here there is no State church, and, whatever advantages a perfect equality of religious societies may be supposed to secure, there is the disadvantage to national manners arising out of the absence of one of the most powerful causes of reverence for, at least, the framework of religion. This disadvantage is not glaringly apparent in this colony at present. But it is reasonable to suppose that, in the course of time, similar effects will be produced here to those which in the United States have followed the absence of a State Church. It will be observed that the question of the merits of the State church system in relation to either religion or morals is avoided, except so far as manners may mean morals.

We have said there is no State church in South Africa. There is however, Schedule C. Now, Schedule C. is a delicate subject, and must in these pages, at least, be handled with tenderness. Let it be assumed that the ecclesiastical grants are of importance to the churches which enjoy them, of importance to religious instruction, and of importance in whatever other way that their advocates maintain, what is their relation to the sentiment of reverence for religion? Were it in the nature of things—ecclesiastical, social, and political—possible that Schedule C. could do its work of distribution without observation, it might, by helping to increase the revenue of public worship, and by thus adding to the respectability of the endowed churches, be friendly to the maintenance of reverence. But this unfortunate schedule drags so much of religion as may be associated with it into the arena of political discussion every year. It places religion in the pillory of the hustings and on the floor of both Houses, where around it rage all the passions of ecclesiastico-political strife,—passions which are undignified and petty, whatever may be the seriousness and magnitude of the principles involved in the quarrel. This state of things cannot promote reverence for religion, although we by no means say that on that account the ecclesiastical grants must be abandoned.

The Cape is not a little remarkable for the multiplicity of its religious and ecclesiastical sects. The influence the pervading presence of heathenism and the existence of Mohammedanism at some of our chief towns may have on the national regard for religion, and especially for the Christian religion, is a question too subtle for us. It is, we think, matter of experience that such a condition of things as that we have here is pretty certain to produce either exclusiveness and the persecuting spirit, or a certain freedom of manner towards religion bordering on laxity, and sometimes going to the length of indifference. In those great Asiatic countries where small bodies of Europeans live in the heart of vast pagan communities, whose religions are as elaborate as their civilizations, these opposite tendencies are very marked. Hindooism, for instance, causes some of its Christian rulers to be bigots, while others it causes to be latitudinarians.

The presence of a religion in which they do not believe, but in which the great majority about them do most earnestly believe, a religion which has in it much that is good, and which, whether good or bad, is a splendid product of the human mind, favours what is known by the name of "liberalism" in religion, which is not always accompanied by a reverence for their own inherited faith.

Heathenism and Mohammedanism in South Africa can scarcely be suspected of having any such decided influence, but that they should exert some influence of the kind is at least possible. We turn from this speculation to facts and influences, whose tendencies as well as whose character can be readily understood. Nowhere, except, perhaps, in America, do Christian sects rejoice in a greater variety than in this colony. The two nationalities, Dutch and English, preserve sacredly their peculiar ecclesiastical institutions, and the teeming womb of Protestantism in Great Britain and Holland has given to this scanty community all its motley births. Then, also, we have Presbyterianism from Scotland and Roman Catholicism from Ireland, while France, Germany, Scandinavia, and America have contributed by their missions to give to the white and seamless garment of Christ the look of a coat of many colours and of many patches. Private judgment, independent thought, the authority of the personal conscience, toleration, are phrases beyond criticism, as they are precious things that cannot be assailed. Yet they are of that great value in themselves that they are not to be endangered by any discovery that in their operations and embodiment they are attended by certain drawbacks. Yet these drawbacks ought to be noted and removed as far as possible. Division, so far as it lessens in anything the quantity of size, lessens that which commands respect. Other things being present, a Christian society, comprehending all within its ample circle, would impress the imagination and ensure reverence in a degree unknown under the present circumstances of perplexing division. The unity of the faith is a much grander thing than variety of opinion, however the various facets of this much-lauded jewel may sparkle and glow with iridescent rays. It is not, however, the simple facts of division which so much militate against a reverence for religion as the rivalries, jealousies, and uncharitableness which are the too common elements of sectarian life, and which prevail the more in inverse proportion to the smallness of the disjointed community. Few things make religion look more unlovely and less dignified than the squabbles of schools, the hatred between parties, and the strife of sects. The Christian clansman may respect religion in his own Church, but he despises it in another; and thus his reverence is mixed with the base alloy of selfishness, and, in fact, ceases to be reverence, which in its very essence is the subordination of self to the object venerated. No charge is made against any one church, or any group of churches, in this colony. We have used generalities in order to avoid what is not intended. The object of these remarks is to ask attention to the almost certain influence of the remarkable number of churches in this country.

There is another consideration to be advanced in connection with reverence for religion, which, however difficult in itself, cannot well be avoided. We refer to the influence of all that can only be expressed by "Colensoism,"—not, however, to the whole influence of that fact of the day and of our place, but to a lateral influence which it is possibly calculated to exert. It is the singular lot of British South Africa to be the home of the man and the ecclesiastic who in modern times has given the most practical effect to the great Protestant principle of free private judgment in matters deemed sacred. It is no part of our duty to value the methods or the results of Bishop Colenso's labours. There is no necessity for us to call him heretic, or to call him reformer—to condemn, or to applaud. With us the task is to see whether the fact of the celebrated critic being one of us, and doing his work here, taken together with the incidents of the ecclesiastical struggle in which he is the central figure, and by which he naturally attracts to himself some sympathy and much ardent partisanship, is not likely to have an effect not wholly favourable on the popular regard for religion. The question is not whether the studies, investigations, and conclusions of the bishop are likely to make him irreverent. In all probability they do not. We should regret to think they did. In an essay personal experience is admissible, and the writer in this case would be sorry to erase the impressions of his youth and the knowledge of after years concerning this great man—great, at any rate. Following him at a public school, we found the name of "John William Colenso" printed in gilded letters on a tablet which included the names of all the scholars who had won honours and were worthy of emulation. Since then we have heard him teach in his cathedral, with lips breathing lovingkindness to man and devotion to God, and have seen the modest palace midst the tumbled hills eastward from Maritzburg, where, with an untiring and unambitious zeal, he spent so much of his life in the humble but arduous work of a mere missionary. And we find it difficult to suppose otherwise than that, whatever his work, his motives are honest and unselfish, and his spirit towards religion devout, devoted, and full of worship. We are insinuating nothing against the author, or against his books. Neither are we attempting to consider whether the tendency of his writings is to foster irreverence among those who are themselves able to judge them by the test of accumulated learning and sound manly reason, and who may accept them as contributions to human discovery in the Divine and, therefore, mysterious Word. It is possible to believe that such disciples may preserve their respect for the faith, whose depository their Master has taught them to handle without what to them appears to be a superstitious dread. The case we are to consider is this: A bishop startles the world with books which contain strange investigations and bold conclusions on a subject hitherto held to be sacred—at least to bishops. By an accident, this prelate rules a South African see. He is a colonist—a South African colonist. This launches his books upon the colonies, gets them a local circulation amongst persons and classes of persons with whom, had there been no relationship of place, such literature would have found no acceptance. The books, it may be, are but little read, less studied, still less understood; but through allusions in the newspaper press, and by the mouth of rumour and shallow, sounding talk, the bare and bald but bold conclusions of an elaborate process of criticism get a lodgment in the common mind; and knowing how scant is the learning of the colony in the departments of biblical, philological, historical, or other criticism, as well as how little accustomed are the majority to really exercise their own judgment; knowing also how great a proneness there is in these days to loose thinking on questions of religion, and how welcome to the flippant would be the seeming authority of a great church dignitary; is there not reason for supposing that all this would be pretty sure to encourage an irreverent temper towards religion? Anon the bishop is declared to be a heretic, the effect of which, in some quarters, is to make heresy respectable, especially so as everywhere in South Africa this heretical bishop is renowned for his zeal and respected for his learning. At the next stage he is excommunicated, and his bishopric is given to another. This makes him a martyr, and fires the sympathies of many, who, in embracing the cause of the man and the officer, become attached to his views, which, however, they are more likely to misunderstand than to comprehend, and which, when received without intelligence, cannot, it is to be feared, but conduce to irreverence. If it be the case that the painful labours of his later years should, however indirectly, contribute to bring religion into disrespect among the colonists of South Africa, we believe no one would deplore so evil a result more than the bishop himself.

We have now reviewed some of the causes which may possibly favour, perhaps, the most serious form of irreverence in the South African colonies; and with this closes an essay which may itself be charged with the fault it has endeavoured to exhibit. It is possible to exaggerate evils and to distort facts and national characteristics by insisting upon looking at them through the medium of a foregone theory. Much that has been said may seem to be the result of a want of respect for South Africa. As yet, as we have already said, there is not much fervour of nationality or true patriotism amongst any of us. But this much may be ventured, that national character in most new countries early takes the form of vainglory. The best corrective of this is the discipline of criticism, which, however, should not be ill-natured, and we hope in this case it is, at least, free from that fault.

LOOKING-GLASSES.

A Lecture delivered in Grahamstown.

What I wish to do in this paper is to give a few illustrations of that wonderful activity of representation which, in this nineteenth century, places before men and things, appearances and events, a multitude of mirrors, amongst which the genuine looking-glass takes a very inferior place indeed, but of which it may nevertheless be taken to be suggestive if not typical.

All of us who have moved about the world with our eyes open must have observed, what glass manufacturers, cabinet makers, house decorators, and furniture dealers could tell us as matter of trade statistics, that looking-glasses—mirrors of the vulgar sort—are in much greater demand and in more general and varied use now than at any time before. Whether the world is growing vainer as it grows older, or whether it is desirous of obeying the command, "Man, know thyself," and wants to know, you know, I will not venture to say—nor will I venture to say whether it is or is not snobbishly characteristic of what some one has lately called the "snobbish nineteenth century;" but it is an undeniable fact that looking-glasses have increased, are increasing, and have spread themselves over the world of late to an extent surpassed only by the almost miraculous distribution of beer-bottles. It has been estimated, I will not say how truly, that the streets of London could be paved and repaved with the existing pier-glasses, and that a dozen Crystal Palaces could be built of the pocket-mirrors now in use. Public rooms, hotels, clubs, shops, the saloons of steamers, and the waiting-rooms of railway stations, are lined with mirrors. Much furniture is panelled with plate glass and quicksilver. Wardrobes and sideboards are made of as much glass as wood. In most modernly equipped rooms you find at least "six Richmonds in the field." Mirrors are made to do detective duty in jewellers' shops; they are useful in jails as spies; and they find their way, so it is said, into churches. There are some who are malicious enough to say that the reason why so many men, on entering our temples, bury their faces in their hats, is that they have cunningly fixed in the crown a little looking-glass, and that the deity they worship with so much apparent devotion is a neat though small image of themselves.

But let us not waste time over that which, although perfectly reflecting everything presented to it, retains nothing and adds nothing to the stock of the world's knowledge, or of our knowledge of the world. Were it in my power to present to every one a looking-glass, I am aware that every one would have before him a more agreeable subject and object than any I can introduce; but, while every one would find his pleasure increased by the contemplation of himself, who could say that the circle of his information was very much enlarged? Looking-glasses fail to circulate their impressions. It would be useless for a lover to gaze tenderly into a looking-glass and then send it as a present to his mistress, with the fond but foolish hope that it would convey to her the touching expression of his sentiments. There is, I doubt not, in the possession of some one the identical bit of glass in which Napoleon shaved on the morning of Waterloo. But the fortunate curiosity collector, when he looks into it, sees nothing but the smug image of himself. On the French coast from time to time possibly some fragments of the wrecked steamer *London* will be washed up, and, may be, amongst the drift will be a piece of a saloon mirror, such as we see in those ships of size, but if so it will bear no trace or shadow of the pale faces that it reflected on that sad day when so many slid beneath the wave. The little child who, gathering shells, picks up, perchance, the piece of glass, will see therein only its own wide eyes and sunny locks tumbled by the wind. I can think of nothing from a distant home that would remind one less of the place it came from than a looking-glass, and just because, like some poor toady who has changed patrons, it would reflect its new surroundings and seem to be a part of them, while of the old associations it would have no memory.

It is very different with the photograph.

Were we asked what one of all the wonderfully active agencies engaged in the work of representation in the present day was the most active, I think we should all be likely, whether rightly or not I will not say, to reply, "The photograph." The photograph seizes the truth—that part of the truth of form and appearance which comes within its domain—seizes the truth, holds it, communicates it, circulates it throughout the world, treasures it up for the future, perpetuates the truth of to-day, as the sun sees it and writes it, through the succession of to-morrows during which the same sun will continue its annals now that it has begun this new style of history writing.

Let us observe that the photograph entirely belongs to the present, passing age. So far as this, at all events, the nineteenth century is one of the Light Ages; inasmuch as in it "light" is for the first time, in this remarkably direct way, pressed into the service of representing the truth as it is in form. I have nothing to do with photography as an art, or with its place in art, or with its relations to science; my duty is simply to exhibit it as an agent of representation—as a looking-glass doing more than looking-glass ever did.

For this purpose let us form an estimate, if we can, of the extent to which the art is practised and its works distributed. We have but scanty statistics, and it would be ridiculous to think of counting the host of the servants who wait upon the sun. A reviewer who wrote nearly twenty years ago grew eloquent upon the progress photography had made in the fifteen years it had then been known. "Since," said he, "the day when the first cloudy specimens in bistre of a new and mysterious art were first exhibited to our wondering gaze, photography has become a household word and a household want; it is used alike by art and science, by love, business, and justice; is found in the most sumptuous saloon and in the dingiest attic, in the solitude of the mountain cottage and in the glare of the London gin-palace, in the pocket of the detective, in the cell of the convict, in the folio of the painter and architect, among the papers and patterns of the mill-owner and manufacturer, and on the cold brave breast on the battle-field."

Twenty years ago, when the art was still in its young and tender years, the London Directory had column after column of its closely packed pages devoted to the whereabouts of photographic artists. Then it was possible for enthusiastic writers to ask, "Who can number the legion of petty dabblers, who display their trays of specimens along every great thoroughfare of every great town? What out-of-the-way hamlet is too much out of the way to be visited by the photographic travelling van?" So long ago as 1857 it was possible to say that in England alone tens of thousands were following a new business, practising a new pleasure, speaking a new language, and bound together by a new sympathy. And if all this could be said of the great activity with which the art was then practised, what could be said now that nearly twenty years have increased its appliances, widened its dominion, perfected its processes, and added to its votaries?

The men in the higher ranks of the calling are far more plentiful than doctors, and nearly as numerous as lawyers; while in the lower walks, the photographic "hartists," as Punch calls them, are as legion. Henry Mayhew's street photographic friend said, " I have been told that there are near upon 250 houses in London now getting a livelihood taking sixpenny portraits. There's ninety of 'em I'm personally acquainted with, and one man I know has ten different shops. There's eight in the Whitechapel Road alone, from Butcher Row to Mile End Turnpike. Bless you, yes! they all make a good living of it."

But it is notorious that photography is emphatically the amateur's art. For every man who wins his bread by this means, there are at least a score who make it their hobby. There is not, I venture to say, a person who reads this who does not know half a dozen friends and acquaintances who dabble in negatives and positives, talk of collodion and calotype, and make their fingers dirty with nitrate of silver. Half of us at least know what it is to be taken off by an enthusiastic neighbour who has a little burning hot sentry-box in his back yard, in which he insists upon making us sit every time there is "a splendid light to-day—by Jupiter, a most splendid light!" And there is no rank or class in life free from these terribly earnest photographers. Sometimes it happens that the first man in the place is a devoted admirer of the art; and in that case photography becomes at once an endemic. Everybody catches it. Everybody practises on everybody else. When I was in Natal once, it so happened that the Governor was an amateur photographer. What was the result? Everybody was either taking or being taken. The whole colony was being arranged into interesting groups for the camera. As a matter of course the heads of the departments followed their chief, and as an equal matter of course the tails of the departments followed the heads. It went through the civil service as the influenza goes through a family; then it spread to the military; and thence to the laity. When Mr. Wilson, the gentleman who brought the process called Sennotype to this colony and who himself was one of its originators, was here, he told me that the Emperor of Brazil was a most ardent photographer, and that he had bought the Sennotype secret. We may be sure, therefore, that in Brazil photography is another word for loyalty, and that every third man has his camera. But everywhere this art has its patrons, giving it the prestige of great names and adding fashion to its attractions. The Emperors of Russia and Austria, adopting the old way of paying for new debts, are bestowing snuff-boxes on photographic merit. Her Majesty the Queen some time ago sent out a complete photographic apparatus to the King of Siam. A peer of France offers a little fortune in photographic prizes; the name of the Primate of England figures on the committee of a photographic association; the Lord Chief Baron of the Exchequer is the president of the first photographic society. The Council of King's College have instituted a lectureship of photography; photographic establishments are attached to the Royal Arsenal at Woolwich; the Royal Artillery and Engineers have their photographic classes; and the Royal Institution has its photographic studies. Photographic societies are to be found in all countries, and in England alone there are half a dozen photographic newspapers. It will be seen from this rapid sketch that what has been called "the social apparatus" of this wonderful art is itself wonderfully complete.

An article in *Macmillan* assures us that ladies and gentlemen may qualify themselves to take views all by themselves, by a process which can be learnt in a quarter of an hour, and with an amount of apparatus that the gentlemen could carry in their coat-pockets, and the ladies in their reticules. By this means anybody may take anybody out-of-doors. By another contrivance, I find, photography is possible within the very bosom of families on the shortest notice. In the Bookseller's Catalogue, I met with the following advertisement: "A New Wonder; or Instantaneous Photography in the Drawing-Room. Retail price 1s. The packet contains material for three photographs, with three developers, and three cards for mounting." Then follow criticisms from the newspapers.

The *Standard* says: "Any person by this extraordinary process can produce in a few moments a perfect photograph. The effect is really wonderful."

The *City Press* with much effusion declares that "the effect is perfectly magical."

The advertisement closes with the notice: "The demand for this novelty is so immense that a day or two's delay in the execution of orders must be pardoned."

What limit is there to the representative power of an art like this—an art which can press into its service not only a multitude of regular practitioners who earn their living by its means, but chief barons, tradesmen, governors, peers, peasants, the prince of the blood royal, the serving-man, Cambridge wranglers, archbishops, curates, emperors, and parish-beadles—an art which puts its machinery into a coat-pocket and can perform its wonders in a few minutes on a drawing-room carpet—an art which has the luminous arch of the firmament for its laboratory, the exhaustless fount of light for the supply of its chief material, and the sun for its chief minister—an art which can in one moment, by the simplest and the grandest means, stamp the likeness of a human face in all the varied beauty or horror of its expression; which can fix the dropping of a child's tear, and the fall of an avalanche; pencil the down upon a baby's cheek, and the bristling pine forests of a Norway precipice; paint the delicate, tiny flower half hidden in its leaves, and the leafless Burnham beeches in a winter landscape; the latest palace with the scaffolding yet unremoved, and the ruin in its latest stage of decay; the wounds of the dead soldier lying as he fell upon the field, and the welcome of the conqueror as he passes to the capitol; the faces of the absent, the homes we have left, the graves of the departed; which can arrest the murderer in his flight, confronting him although he may have crossed the ocean, and comfort the solitary exile with its life-like copies of a mother's smile; which with a marvellous fidelity can reproduce the text of a precious manuscript, or copy Sinaitic carvings, cuneiform inscriptions, the hieroglyphics of Carnac, the inscriptions of Persepolis, or the outlines of a Buddhist temple in Ceylon; which can multiply truthful fac-similes of all that the great masters built or carved, painted or cast; all that modern genius wielding the mighty modern forces can accomplish—the launch of a *Northumberland*, the infinitely varied collections of a Great Exhibition, the shining walls of a Crystal Palace, the leaping arch of a bridge, the pillars of a temple, and the snaky coils of an ocean telegraph; which, descending, can bring to light the bed of the ocean, and which, ascending, can paint the caverns of the moon, and sketch the form of the curious horns which shoot out from the sun's edge during an eclipse? What limit is there to the achievements of an art like this? With what ever-increasing power shall it copy all that the eye can see or light irradiate, and with what activity shall it accumulate its transcripts of phenomena and events through the long future, during which its processes shall be more and more accurate, and its mastery over the visible more and more despotic?

What an agency of representation have we in illustrated periodical literature, which, considering the avidity with which they are borrowed as well as bought, their popularity in reading-rooms, and the care with which they are preserved, may be reckoned to have a wider circulation than anything issued from the press. What event of any importance happens in any part of the world, let it be a battle in which mighty armies are engaged, or a competitive exhibition of pigs; the launch of the *Leviathan*, or the invention of a mousetrap; the eruption of a volcano, or the blaze of a bonfire; the death of a hero, or the execution of a criminal; the horrors of a revolution, or a town-and-gown row; the latest masterpiece of art, or the newest thing in fashion; the great Reform debate, or the last prize-fight; a Lord Mayor's feast, or feeding-time in the Zoological Gardens,—what event is there that has the least publicity which is not fashioned by these periodicals into a picture, and distributed broadcast throughout the world? And the same may be said of topographical scenes and the portraits of eminent or notorious men, the views of buildings, and pictures of costumes, customs, habit, and manner of life.

Sometimes a statement of details will convey a truer or livelier impression of magnitude than the most precise definition or widest generalization. Thus there are men who can form no adequate comprehension of a quart bottle of wine until they have poured it out into fifteen wine-glasses. Recognizing this, I have had the curiosity and taken the trouble to copy down the subjects illustrated in one month's number of the *News*. They are as follows, taken in the order in which they appear in the paper:—" Christ Church National School, Battersea—The Albert Memorial Hospital, Wollongong, Sydney—A Burmese bell—Benhilton Church. Surrey—Memorial Church, New South Wales—War-dance of New Zealanders—War-canoes racing—The Thames Embankment—Divine Service on board the *Indefatigable*— The *Indefatigable* herself—" Tuning up," by Johnson—The funeral procession of the late Queen of the French—Installation of the New Master of Trinity College—Punikha, Bhoolan—The burnt palace of the Rajah of Lalaka— Garibaldi memorial—Mr. Peabody giving prizes—Passion and Patience—General Burgoyne—The late Rev. John Keble—Installation of Mr. Carlyle—The launch of the *Northumberland*—Review at Brighton—The Grand Stand—Regatta at Singapore—St. Helena with troop-ship at anchor—London street improvements—Rescue of eleven seamen—Lord Lyon, winner of the 2000-guinea stakes, Newmarket—Animals taking refuge from a prairie fire—Wakefield Exhibition prize medal—Eastport, Maine, U.S.—Westminster Hall on the night of the division on the Reform debate—Sir Mark Cubbon's Statue at Bangalore, India—Paris fashions—Royal Surrey Hospital—Launch of the life-boat at Oxford—Regent Street in the Season—Brisbane, Queensland—The Royal Memorial Arch—East India United Club House—Bust of Thackeray—Spring, a statue—European quarter of Zanzibar—Five views of Bamberg—Ivory and skin sale in the Grahamstown market—The Glasgow University—A spring shower, near the Exchange—The New Palace Yard on the day Mr. Gladstone moved the second reading of the Reform Bill—The City Lunatic Asylum—Funeral of one of the fire-brigade—Race at Epsom—Taking in the pictures at the Royal Academy—Bamborough Castle—Scene from the favourite of Fortune—The King of Siam in state costume—Amazons of the King of Siam—Victoria, Hong Kong—Panama—Cemetery and race course, Hong Kong—Summer garden at St. Petersburg—Old College of Physicians—Garrison Church, Fort William, Calcutta—The font of the Protestant Church at Naples."

I scarcely should have believed that one month's number of a single pictorial periodical contained so many views unless I had thus tested the case. Think, then, of the accumulated representations of a year, of their wide distribution—remember that we have but noted the performance of one paper, that in England there are several, that there is not a nation in Europe which has not its picture papers, that the United States abound with them, that some of our Australian colonies have them—and then form an estimate of the mirroring power and activity of this agency! And let us, in passing, record the fact that the pictorial newspaper is another birth of the nineteenth century.

And within the same period to what a marvellous extent has descriptive literature, the literature of travel, of natural history, of science generally, of art, of mechanics, been enriched and explained by pictures! What Livingstone saw, as he stood under the drenching spray of the Zambesi Falls, he shows us by the help of the engraver's art. We can thus watch with Speke the Nile as it flows full and free from the long unknown lake. We should all of us know a gorilla, were we to meet one, from his portrait in Du Chaillu's book. Hooker has placed us near the snowy peaks of Himalaya. Ruskin has made us familiar with the stones of Venice. There is a picture-gallery devoted wholly to ferns, and another to fungi. What insect is there that has not its portrait? The infinitely little things to which mites are monsters have been magnified into sight by the microscope, and their shape fixed for ever by the pencil, and given to the naked eye. Is there not now a map of the moon in the school books on astronomy? If not for worship, yet for knowledge, men make unto themselves graven images of the things in heaven, the things on earth, and the things under the earth.

Even art itself—the painter's art—nowadays largely devotes itself to the representation of the present, and that school which loves the past loves also to be literal and true. Ruskin says of pre-Raphaelitism that it has but one principle, that of absolute uncompromising truth in all that it does, obtained by working everything, down to the most minute detail, from nature, and from nature only. Every pre-Raphaelite landscape background is painted to the last touch, in the open air, from the thing itself. Every pre-Raphaelite figure, however studied in expression, is a true portrait of some living person. Every minute accessory is painted in the same manner. This—this devotion to the representation of the truth—is the main pre-Raphaelite principle.

I cannot take leave of this kind of looking-glass which aims at reproducing the forms and semblances of things, and the very action of events, without a reference to that wonderfully true mirror of the times—modern caricature. In the hands of men like the younger Doyle, John Tenniel, and the lamented John Leech, caricature is no lie or libel, but the truest truth. Where else but in their sketches do we see the very men and women—the life and manner of the day? Leech is dead, but his art lives, and with it how much that is characteristic of this century. Its horses and horsemen, as one said before he died, good riders and bad, exquisite dandies and vulgar snobs, citizens and country bumpkins, old-fashioned English gentlemen and naughty boys, footmen and maid-servants, blooming young ladies and elderly matrons, are all depicted with equal fidelity and spirit. The beauty, gracefulness, and nature of his women have never been approached. His celebrated Briggs series alone is a whole furniture shop full of looking-glasses, in which, if the whole tribe of Briggses do not see themselves, the whole world sees the tribe. Punch is a sad scamp. He laughs consumedly. He is an irreclaimable quiz. But he tells no fibs. His mask is transparent. And truth lies at the bottom of his bowl. I take it, that of all the looking-glass makers of this looking-glass century, Punch turns out one of the faithfulest and most polished piece of work there is.

This is the age of photography; the age of pictures; the age of elaboration and truth in art. It is also the age of great and little exhibitions—the age of shows! And herein we find our next looking-glass. These institutions —for they are such—are, I know, competitive; but that is only one of their chief characteristics. They are also representative. They exhibit samples of the products, the raw materials, the manufactures, the commodities, the inventions, the successes, which Nature's industry, skill, and genius have given to civilization. They show the choicest of these things, so that when a man looks at one of these vast and varied collections he sees, as in a mirror, the wealth of the world—wealth of material in the land, the sea, the air; in the mine, the soil, the forest, and in the creature that hath life—wealth of invention, application, labour, patience, perseverance, in man—wealth of utility, of luxury, of art and science—universal wealth. I am speaking now of such truly great exhibitions as that in London in 1851, again in 1861; as that in Dublin, in Munich, in Manchester, in Florence, and New York, and as that which is to overtop all others at Paris. It must be remembered that these shows are as remarkable for their minuteness of representation as well as for their full-orbed mirroring. They aim at the most careful classification. There are departments and sub-departments. In their entirety of accumulation, they display the whole circle of human achievement as far as the products of industry are concerned. But then they also show in long lines of successive courts what the physical endowment and genius of each nation have contributed to the great sum total of triumph. To those temples dedicated to brotherhood, knowledge, and progress, the tribes of the earth come up and lay their offerings each one in its place, under its own territorial badge and national banner. So that the crowds behold as they pass along the distinctive productions of each country's soil and the peculiar industrial and artistic results of each country's genius. These exhibitions are the parliaments of labour, and the representation is wide as mankind. The suffrage is universal, and only those are excluded who shut out themselves. Then again, by the action of the other principle of competition, there is introduced into these exhibitions the classification according to kind, so that spectators may see at the same time what the world and men have accomplished in one sphere of labour with the same materials.

But the sample-showing spirit of the age is by no means confined to the great exhibitions which now and then reflect full-orbed the circle of the world's industry and wealth. What almost countless numbers of local and departmental exhibitions there are! This colony of ours, which cares so little to take its part in the cosmopolitan displays of great European cities, is an illustrious example of the rage for local shows. In this province alone about twenty agricultural exhibitions are held annually, at which our flocks and herds, our cereals and dairy produce, our pickles and preserves, and, above all, our wool, are represented and re-represented with a pertinacity that would be wearisome if it were not useful. The Bay has its yearly wool show, and Alice is to have its yearly mohair show, and Grahamstown its yearly flower and fruit show. And that which is seen in this colony to be so characteristic of the day and the place, is everywhere characteristic. Nor is this activity of representation limited to agriculture. In the poor and crowded parts of London, the mechanic shows the model of some ship or machine, the making of which has solaced his evenings; the sempstress exhibits the flower, bedded in a spoutless teapot, which she has reared on her window-sill midst smoke and dust; and the young genius of the alley displays the drawing at which he has worked in the hours stolen from play. Then, who shall count the exhibitions of art in all its branches—of machinery, of scientific experiment? Dog shows have of late become fashionable. Not long ago in America—where else?—there was a baby show! While it was but the other day that the barbers of Paris exhibited themselves and their profession in public, and cut hair and built chignons before an array of spectators. This desire to exhibit things shows itself in nothing more strikingly than in the growing width and height and clearness of shop-windows and the multiplying of show-rooms.

My next looking-glass is the mirror of statistics. All things nowadays are enumerated and represented by figures. The whole world and all it contains are being turned into tables. Do we not know it by personal experience? Did not that troublesome Parliament of ours a year or two ago pass a Census Act? And did not a set of Paul Prys, armed with the very pointed clauses of that act, invade our castles, and demand to know how many of us there were; our ages; whether we were able to read or write; whether we were coloured persons or not; who of us were blind, or deaf, or dumb, or lunatic, or foolish? Did they not want to know what strangers slept within our gates on a certain night, and how many cattle, horses, mules, and pigs we kept? The Cape has caught this mania for figures. But, as yet, we have taken it very mildly, and our own experience affords us but little idea of how it rages elsewhere.

In France, where organization and system are carried out to a wonderful nicety of perfection, in Belgium and in Prussia, every fact that a detective and inquisitorial statistical police can capture is seized and allotted to its place in some class of facts; and everything that can be numbered is represented by a figure. In those countries there is nothing the man is or has or has not, which is not tabulated. His age, his calling, his education, his place of birth, his place of residence, his children, his servants, his name, the number of his limbs, the condition of his senses, his diseases, and the state of his mind, are all noted and registered. Then all these facts about the individual man are collated with the same sort of facts about all the men in the nation, and thus groups of facts are formed representing the great truths and forces of national life—presenting to the statesman, the political economist, the philosopher, the physician, the philanthropist, the priest, and the policeman, mirrors in which they may behold the conditions of humanity with which they have to deal.

In England the government is less paternal, and John Bull likes not to be too much watched and looked after, and thus facts as well as persons there have greater liberty. But there, also, Paul Pry is at his work. Let me give two or three illustrations. Dr. Milroy, in his statement on the utilizing of statistics of disease among the poor, says that upwards of 3000 medical officers are, under the General Superintendence of the Poor Law Board, engaged in keeping registers of each case coming before them. The second illustration of the activity of representation displayed by statisticians is the curious but suggestive fact that one inquiring mind has made it his duty to calculate the number of sermons preached yearly in London. He has discovered that number to be no less than four millions. Like some mirrors, statistics often distort, instead of represent, facts, and the figures they yield are occasionally grotesquely absurd. Will any one who has read "The Chimes," that most famous of Dickens's Christmas Stories, forget the laughable caricature of the man of facts and figures, Mr. Filer? Trotty Veck, you will remember, is in the blissful enjoyment of a dish of smoking hot tripe, which he is eating on a door-step, when there burst forth upon him Mr. Filer and Alderman Cute.

"'Who eats tripe?' said Mr. Filer, looking around. 'Tripe is, without exception, the least economical, and the most wasteful article of consumption that the markets of this country can by possibility produce. The loss upon a pound of tripe has been found to be, in the boiling, seven-eighths of a fifth more than the loss upon a pound of any other animal substance whatever. Taking into account the number of animals slaughtered yearly within the bills of mortality alone, and forming a low estimate of the quantity of tripe which the carcases of those animals, reasonably well butchered, would yield, I find that the waste on that amount of tripe, if boiled, would victual a garrison of five hundred men for five months of thirty-one days each, and a February over. The waste, the waste! You snatch your tripe, my friend, out of the mouths of widows and orphans. Divide the amount of tripe before mentioned by the estimated number of existing widows and orphans, and the result will be one pennyweight of tripe to each. Not a grain is left for this man. Consequently, he's a robber.'

"Trotty was so shocked, that it gave him no concern to see the alderman finish the tripe himself. It was a relief to get rid of it, anyhow."

This piece of exaggeration represents no actual truth, but it indicates in its own way the length to which statistical inquiry is pushed. It aims at the most minute calculation with regard to number, value, size, weight, force, and every physical and economical attribute of every *thing*, as well as of the properties and faculties of every *being*.

From the perfection to which the art of counting has been brought, it will soon no longer be hyperbolical to talk of numbering the hairs on the head, the stars of heaven, or the sand upon the sea-shore.

My last looking-glass is representative literature.

In a great and wide sense all literature is representative —a mirror of the minds which produce it, or of the subjects concerning which it treats. Did I feel myself able or at liberty to follow out this view, this paper would never come to a close, for, as the wise king said long ago, of the making of books there is no end. Solomon said that when, probably, all the books in the world could be held in the smallest room in his palace. What would he say now, were he to see the flood of printed matter which with unceasing, with ever-increasing flow, deluges the world! In the time of Horace it was a complaint that there were too many writers. In the days of Shakespeare, and again in those of Pope, the intolerable number of gentlemen who insisted upon giving birth to books was a perpetual subject of jest. Forty years ago, a cynical tourist, meeting Sir

Walter Scott in a stage coach, and being charmed with his conversation during the journey, expressed his delight that at last he had fallen in with a sensible man who had never published a book. What would those critics of bygone and comparatively bookless times say now that this globe of ours could be wrapped up in printed paper, and that every tenth man you meet is more or less an author! Were it possible for me to display the mirror-like properties of universal literature, and were I to do it, the effect would be similar to that which is produced when a mischievous boy dexterously reflects from a looking-glass the whole blaze of the sun into the blinded eyes of a passer-by. Such a thing I cannot do, and will not attempt. My task is simply to specify the especial departments of modern literature which are devoted to the representation of the facts of human life and condition.

I will say nothing about blue-books, parliamentary papers, and the evidence taken before parliamentary committees. There is a popular prejudice against this species of literature. But let the truth be told. Just as in the dark and dismal caverns and black, opaque masses of a coal mine we find the very substance of light, so these books, so dull and dry, so heavy and hideously thick, contain some of the truest representations of some of the most important political, economical, and social aspects of passing human life. But I forbear. To attempt to prove that a blue-book is a looking-glass would be an act of madness of which I am not capable. Equal sense will I display by shunning everything but the names of those perfect and all-comprehensive reflectors—encyclopædias. I will not do more than remind you of those curious volumes which find so many purchasers, "Enquire Within," "Five Millions of Facts," "The Year-Book of Facts." Let these and their companions whose name is legion pass, and let us spend a portion of the few minutes left to us in briefly noticing that department of modern literature which concerns itself about the poor.

It must have been recognized by us in this colony, who have so little to do practically with this kind of literary mirroring, that of late years an extraordinary amount of thought, care, and inquiry have been devoted to the discovery and exhibition of the state of the lower, and especially of the very lowest, classes of European society. This I take to be one of the most satisfactory signs of the times. As a fact of literature it is one which gladdens the heart and lightens the labour of the humblest man who drives the most spluttering and bluntest quill. Until lately the misery, the privations, the struggles, the crime, the wonderful shifts and dodges resorted to to keep life from the hand of death ever near, the whole natural history of the poor, have been hidden away in the dangerous quarters, the back slums, the horrible holes and corners of great cities. But some writers have felt it to be their duty to explore those unknown interiors, and returning to the upper circles, they have shown as in a glass the strange and sometimes terrible facts they had discovered, and the outlandish or fearful scenes they had witnessed.

This age has been signalized by much splendour of enterprise in the direction of travel. Life has been risked in the solution of the great problems presented by the frozen oceans and the mysterious currents of the North. Solitary men have traced a painful pathway with their feet across the before-unknown zones of this continent of ours; and one has found a river no one knew of; while another has seen the veiled source of a river that was never unknown, but whose fountain-head has been until now the secret of all time. Burke, Wills, and Leichardt died in the act of searching out the central wilds of Australia. Much heroism has been expended on geographical discovery, and the most fascinating books of the day are those that display, in picture and graphic story, the new fields won for knowledge, and redeemed from ignorance by the valour and skill and sacrifice of the traveller. But let us not forget the work of social discovery, and the additions made to the knowledge of man, accomplished by men who have ventured to pass the boundaries which hitherto have divided our Alsatias and our St. Gileses from the pleasant regions of respectability; who have groped for the truth in the foul and hideous sewers where crime, vice, and pestilence are gathered together beneath the heavy, sullen night of ignorance, and who, when they have rescued the truth, have not shrunk from the task of telling it. Such men are those humble city missionaries and others, who enabled Henry Mayhew to compile his wonderful cyclopædia, in many volumes, of the "Condition and Earnings of the London Poor;" the men who gave to Blanchard Jerrold the facts for his "Children of Lutetia" (as his books on the poor of Paris are called); the man who, in the guise of a casual, passed a night of discovery in the casual's ward amongst the refuse of the refuse, and who wrote those articles in the *Pall Mall Gazette* which the whole world has read.

Intimately associated with this kind of literature is that which occupies itself with the exposition of life in our hospitals, our lunatic asylums, and our prisons; and again that which devotes itself to the investigation of the trades, the callings, and the means of livelihood of the labouring classes. From the numerous works which this agency of representation has given us, it is no longer possible to repeat, unmodified, that old saying that half the world does not know how the other half lives. The minuteness of the information as well as its voluminousness, its details as well as its breadth, astonish one. We are introduced into the Sweep's Home, instructed in the natural history of the mud-lark, are made familiar with the rat-catcher of the sewers, and shown the manner of life of the bone-grubber, the crossing-sweeper, and the tramp. You will find in the "Children of Lutetia"—one of the books in our library—all about the poor man's money-lender of Paris, who charges cent. per cent. by lending from sunrise to sunset; about the women who earn their living by going from house to house through the winter nights to wake the sleepers who must be at the markets; about the collectors of old crusts, and the men who grind the old crusts over again and convert them into gingerbread;

the gatherers together of bits of orange and lemon peel which lie about the streets, and those ingenious manufacturers who with the peel so gathered make delicious drinks; and also about those men whom the polite-tongued Parisians call "guardian angels"—the men whose business it is to see drunkards safe home from the wine-shops at the rate of a penny per head.

But there is no mirror of this class like the newspaper. I speak, of course, not of any one broad or narrow sheet, but of the whole product of the newspaper press throughout the world. Consider the machinery at work to collect and arrange and set forth the facts each day brings forth. You know the story of that prince of detectives who is said to have constructed a monster ear which, placed at a point where all the air passages of his prison met, revealed to him the faintest whisper of the captive in the deepest and most distant cell. Well, the press has made such an ear for the world, and by a thousand and a thousand thousand channels of transmission it gathers to itself the eloquence, the rumour, the groans, the sighs, the prayers, the very gossip of mankind. And then what it hears it tells, so that all may know. To what a wonderful perfection is the modern art of shorthand reporting brought! The torrent of words which leaps and falls almost too rapidly for the ear is followed by the faithful pencil, and within a few hours the utterances are fixed as if they were graven with an iron pen upon a rock for ever. The *Times*, on the morning after a great debate, is a miracle of representation.

Nor are the performances of "our own correspondents" and "our special commissioners" less remarkable. You know the custom of the metropolitan press. Let there be an unusual stir of events anywhere—no matter how distant—thither is sent the trusty messenger, who has eyes to see and ears to hear, with strict instructions to find the truth and record it. Is there a fire in the city, or is Vesuvius in a blaze, there is the man with his pencil and note-book. Is there a murder in the suburbs, or a battle near the Black Sea, there is the man with his pencil and his note-book. Is there a tipsy roysterer to be tied down upon a shutter and carried to the lock-up, or is there a mutiny to be stamped out beneath the walls of Delhi and on the plains of Lucknow, there is the man with his pencil and his note-book. Does a coroner go to Chelsea or a Royal Commission to Jamaica, there is the man with his pencil and his note-book—the everywhere present witness, the detective of the press! Then, again, is to be considered the department which represents opinion, worked by the men who have to find out what other men think, what other men feel, and what the public wishes to have said. And then, perhaps, last though not least, is the department of the penny-a-liner, the literary dustman and bone collector—the man whose business it is not to let the veriest rag of truth, the mere offal and garbage of events, the broken crusts and shattered fragments of facts, the floating straws of rumour, and the very echoes of reports, be lost. There is an army of such men in the service of the press—in the service of the world. And great is the service that they render. You recollect the story of the manure merchant. He had a daughter to dower, and he offered the fortunate bridegroom his choice of fifty thousand golden guineas or a dust-heap. The foolish young fellow took the golden guineas. On which the wise old fellow told him that in the dust-heap he had despised lay untold wealth—wealth for the man who owned it, wealth for the fields that would be enriched by it, wealth of harvest and food and capital for generations. Just so is it with the great dust-heap of small paragraphs and ragged facts which the penny-a-liner piles up from day to day; there is the material from which in time to come the historian and the student of mankind shall find perhaps the richest mine of truth—the brightest, clearest mirror of the past.

I have now done. When I commenced this lecture, I had an idea of grouping these mirrors so that some estimate might be formed of their combined reflective power, and we might shape some notion of the almost perfect knowledge of the times they give—the knowledge which

"Lies like a shaft of light across the land,
And like a lane of beams athwart the sea,
Through all the circle of the golden year."

I had some intention, also, of asking what all this activity of representation tended to; whether it be true, as the same great poet tells us, that

"Knowledge comes, but wisdom lingers, and I linger on the shore;
And the individual withers, and the world is more and more."

But when I had got so far, I saw that there was left no time for this; and I have learnt that, let what will be put into a paper of this kind, much more must be left out; and so, humbly trusting that no one here will favour looking-glasses less for anything I have said, I bring my talk to an end.

BELL VOICES.

How would the world wag without bells? It is not in the least likely that the question will ever pass beyond the airy region of fancies. It is possible to imagine a great bell catastrophe—the general cracking of cups—or the universal downfall of clappers; and in that case what confusion dire and detestable would ensue. Would anybody know when to do anything or go anywhere? when to rise up or when to lie down? Still, doubtlessly, there would be "to everything a season, and a time to every purpose under the heaven," but the question would be—When? What endless cross-purposes, unpunctualities, procrastinations, postponements, prematurities, perplexities, disappointments, discordancies, doubts, and surprises would entangle themselves in the web and woof of human life! May the chapter of accidents never include so terrible a calamity. It is not, however, the purpose of this tintinnabulatory article to speculate on what could be done without bells, or what can be done with them; but rather to ring a few changes on the moods and manners of bells. We will venture to attribute to them hearts as well as tongues, sentiment as well as sound—not in the least attempting anything new in so doing. The poets, who find out for us the secrets, the sympathies, the meanings that are in all things, have been the interpreters of bells also. Schiller says:—

> "That offspring of consuming fire,
>   And man's creative hand,
> High from the summit of the spire
>   Shall murmur o'er the land.
> Like flattery's voice, from yonder tower
> Shall speak the genius of the hour,—
> Shall bid the sons of mirth be glad,
> Shall tell of sorrow to the sad,
>   Reflection to the wise;
> Shall add to superstition's fear,
> And peal on rapt devotion's ear
>   The sounds of Paradise,
> And all, his changeful fate brings down
>   On suffering man below,
> Shall murmur from its metal crown,
>   Or be it joy or woe."

What reference is more frequently heard, at evening parties, and elsewhere, chiming from mouths as sweet as the songs they sing, than—

> "Oh! the merry bells, the merry bells?"

Merry enough they are, certain of them; almost too merry for some old church towers we wot of, only held together by the ivy branches. How their venerable sides thrill and throb with the joy-pulses of a wedding chime! How the metallic old fellows chuckle and nudge one another up in the belfry, when they espy upon the pathway the damsel in the orange blossoms and the youth decked out with rose in button-hole! The tenor generally gives the initiative, and, kicking up his heels in an ecstasy, flings out through every chink, crack, and crevice of the old monk-masonry a welcome that, taken up and emphasized by treble and bass, makes other things flutter beside the ivy leaves,— the little heart, for instance, behind the orange blossoms, and the big heart, too, for that matter, that wears the rose buds.

> "Bell! thou soundest merrily
> When the bridal party
> To the church doth hie!"

Edgar A. Poe, a name rapidly approaching the inevitable whitewashing period, tells us what merriment the Sledge Bells keep up among themselves, as they jingle to the pattering trot of the horse over the northern snow and ice fields:—

> "Hear the sledges with the bells—
>   Silver bells!
> What a world of merriment their melody foretells
>   How they tinkle, tinkle, tinkle,
>   In the icy air of night!
> While the stars that oversprinkle
> All the heavens, seem to twinkle
> With a crystalline delight;
> Keeping time, time, time,
> In a sort of Runic rhyme,
> To the tintinnabulation that so musically swells
> From the bells, bells, bells, bells,
>   Bell, bells, bells,
> From the jingling and the tinkling of the bells."

"Merriment" indeed! The lines ring a very bell-frolic in our ears.

There is a particular bell about which it is possible to

have some doubts. It is the Dinner Bell. Is he merry? Much depends, no doubt, upon the dinner; again, much upon the appetite; again, once more, much upon the company. We should hesitate to call that bell merry which, on a raw, damp, dismal day, rings in a shivering wretch to cold mutton. Without reserve, we positively declare that we know nothing among metallic noises more disgusting—no, not even knife-grinding—than the Dinner Bell, when labouring under a fit of dyspepsia; while the knowledge of the fact that the horrid jingle summons us to the torture of a purgatorial repast with solemn bores, dumb mouths, starched necks, supercilious noses, and sleepy eyes, incite us to bell-murder. Not always merry; yet mostly so. Cold mutton and colder dummies are but exceptional experiences after all. Generally there is a no more genial fellow in all belldom than your Dinner Bell. Let him, by some means or other—say by sniffing a whiff from the kitchen, or by catching a sly glance under the dish covers as they go in, or by hearing the table groan—get to know that a hot substantial and a tasty superfluity or two are ready and waiting, and he will straightway burst out into a fit of long, loud, laughing peals most welcome to all it may concern. Yet were we to stop here we should only libel His Jolliness. He can be merry though the fare he advertises be but coarse and not too plentiful. Who so joyous as the working man's Dinner Bell? We call to mind an official clapper that about 12 o'clock used to call out the artisans of one of the royal yards to their mid-day meal. It was nothing particular to the dull sense.

A sort of dot and go one, ding-donggy affair, pulled, too, by a stiff official rope and the hard official hands of a sour-visaged warden. Yet, if faces can be trusted, no bell could have been merrier. As the two thousand hungry men of labour passed beneath its shadow, it clittered and chattered as if it had been made of molten knives and forks with a dash of spoons: a grand orchestra of feeding!

There are some individual bells or sets of bells that by some special jollity of circumstance or disposition have gained a distinguished reputation for merriment. We scarcely know why; perhaps they were blessed by a more than usually jovial bishop in those olden times when priests, high and low, bore about with them and communicated to all they touched a joyous unction; or, just as probably, some rollicking baron, by way of penance for a sinful pleasure, threw into the furnace, from which the hissing metal of these bells flowed into the mould, his huge silver tankard full of laughing echoes and other mirth memories coarse but racy; or may be some court jester, by way of final joke, plunged, quips, quirps, cap, bells, and all, into the molten mass, and so endowed the chimes for ever with his merry ghost. Who can tell? Be the reason what it may, these bells are understood to have a vested right to merriment not to be disputed.

"Hark, the merry Christ Church bells!"

Who so bold as to change the adjective? Should any unlucky wight, in the pride of scepticism, or even speculative philosophy, attempt to do it, the "mighty Tom" and his potent brothers would come down upon him with such a terrible "bob maxium" as would crack his tympanum and muddle his philosophy for ever. Merry they are, were, and ever will be, as long as they are bells at all.

We have already in passing alluded to the Cap and Bell, the grand order insignia, the star and garter, of the ancient and most renowned royal and baronial jester. How could that faithful servitor, perched at the tremulous extremity of the Merry-Andrew's head-gear, help ringing with laughter when his master's sides, and the sides of royalty, and the sides of nobility, and the very hall sides, shook with his master's wit? Of course the little bell couldn't help it, and shook his sides too right well and merrily, as became him.

Shall we put in the Muffin Bell along with the jovial crew? Doubtless in London, just about tea time, in the season—

> "When fallen leaves together flock,
> And gusts begin to squall;
> And suns go down at six o'clock,
> You've heard the Muffin-call."

Well! For ourselves, we are inclined to say not exactly merry; or rather, merry with a difference; merry, but sobered down to something soothing, and chiming in agreeably with the cup of Hyson, the fire-side, the slippers, the all-the-work-of-the-day-over sort of a feeling with which the Muffin Bell is invariably associated. Mark you, also, that this bell knows the secrets that lie hid in the basket beneath the green baize cloth; it hasn't cried muffins so long without knowing what a muffin is, and without acquiring certain muffin tendencies and sympathies; so it rings out softly as though it had a bit of the dough about its clapper. It has no intention whatever to disturb the quiet evening air, should the air be quiet; and when the gusts and squalls, out for a spree, carry its meek tinklings to wrong streets and into doors that never take in muffins, it picks no noisy quarrel; it in no way puts to silence the hissing of the tea-kettle, or the purring of the cat, or the gentle household voices; but comes in so persuasively pleasing that the very butter seems to melt before it feels the fire.

A very extensive class is the Bell Peremptory—of which, perhaps, the most determined is the Doctor's Night Bell. Hark, how it sounds upstairs, right at the very head of the professional couch! How it tosses and shouts, and shouts and tosses! "I will be heard! get up, sir! don't stay to dress! be quick! do be quick! come, don't you hear me! it's a broken leg! a bad case! a fit! it's life or death! get down or I'll——!" So it goes on,—the most despotic bell that ever left a foundry. It is of no use for the unlucky M.R.C.S. to expostulate, or shake his fist at it, or threaten to twist its neck, or even to muffle it with his night-cap; its soul is of the hardest iron, tempered with the most brazen brass.

Not but what there are other autocrats scarcely less wilful;—take, for instance, the Ship's Bell. Bright, immobile, and taciturn, never allowing itself or any one else half a note beyond the hour-units, never moving, nor allowing to be moved, a single metallic muscle besides its tongue, it rules the crew from topmast point to the lowest depths of the hold, turning in and out a thousand men or so at its once and only bidding. A mighty iron-sceptred ruler from the quarter-deck, most terrible to sleepers, skulkers, and slow men of all sorts. Even passengers—great people who have paid their way into state rooms—must obey the bell on pain of sundry penalties and privations.

But the Railway Bell! We most certainly must have forgotten His Most Determined Majesty when we gave the palm of peremptoriness to the Doctor's night warner. Occasionally, the latter functionary condescends to be persuasive—only at the beginning, however, and always under protest: but the Railway Bell never. It scorns all nonsense of that sort. It insists from the very first jingle. It breaks in without ceremony on the most tender adieus, snatching hand from hand, thrusting asunder the most ardent embrace, abbreviating into the veriest fraction of a second the last fond gaze. No tyrant could be more careless of his subject's comfort. That you have a ponderous portmanteau in your hand is nothing whatever to him; "Drop it," he says, "or stay behind!" That you have the gout, or the rheumatism, or left your right leg in the Crimea, is of the smallest moment to this mighty potentate;—"Come, be smart!" it testily cries out. That you have not tasted the dish of soup you have paid for, which the cold winter blast makes an absolute elixir of life, is not of the slightest consequence. "Now, you sir, we're off!" it shouts with impatient gestures. Our heart aches while we think of the innumerable old and middle-aged ladies whose band-boxes have been crushed, and whose pet pugs have been jammed, strangled, or lost through the passionate hurry-scurry of this tormentor, and the probable number of old and middle-aged gentlemen, who, having with great care deposited their railway wrappers, their feet warmers, their elastic cushions, and their furred and many-folded night-caps in a specially selected carriage, find themselves suddenly jostled and jolted off the platform into a cold, bare, boarded, comfortless box, unpleasantly near the coal scuttle or a cattle waggon; and all through the brutal wilfulness of this peremptory bell tyrant.

Of course Packet Bells are ambitious of being peremptory. They try to be, but somehow they do not succeed; the winds do not always bear them out; sometimes the waves are fractious. They ring you on board with an air of vigour, but generally you need not pay the least attention till the steam is up, or the sails flap from the yards.

There is no denying that there are some bells of variable dispositions; uncertain, capricious fellows, scarcely in the same mood from ring to ring. Such, to particularize, is the Visitor's Bell. On any individual day he will run up and down a kind of bell gamut, from the gentlest tinklings, the mere breath of a sound, to the most importunate and hurrisome of noises; change and change about from a sharp, prompt, severe, business-like, all-at-once-and-over burst, to a series of little jerky, hesitating twitterings. We confess we despair of classifying these eccentricities.

Room Bells are of the same chameleon mood. Observe their provoking inconsistency. The father of the family having overslept himself, desires at once his shaving water, and forthwith the bell, the silky tassel of whose "pull" hangs close at hand, this bell, we say, spreads terror and confusion throughout the whole house; people run upstairs, people run downstairs; Jane scalds her hands, Dorothy trips and tumbles, and Susan vows she'll give warning; and all because of that irritable bell. But, observe! The *pater*, with a vicious slash or two, has got through his daily harvesting, and, snatching a hasty breakfast, he hurries off to office; when *mater*, delicate creature, waking from her slumbers, longs for her morning cup of coffee, and straightway the whole dwelling pulses with a silver rippling; down past drawing-room, past dining-room, down into the very kitchen flows the tinkling tide, suffusing cook Dorothy's face with unctuous smiles, filling housemaid Mary's ears with titilating pleasure, rounding off the points of nursery Susan's angles, as running water smooths the pebbles, causing the coffee to flow out melodiously to the magic measure, into the willing cup, and this too—oh, shade of Aladdin's lamp!—from the very identical bell that just now seemed so fearfully querulous! Bell of the Double Mouth!

Some bells there are that have not a soul above business; perfect bells of the age, thoroughly commercial. Such are Exchange Bells, Market Bells, Auctioneers'

Bells. There is also a small party of this genus who attaches himself particularly to shop doors, and sets up a horrible hullaballoo directly the door is touched. He seems to be suspicious in his small trading way; he can't trust you in the shop by yourself, so he screams out— "Master, here's somebody come; make haste or he'll steal something!" Along with other informers, this bell is deservedly "served out." Nobody likes him. Boys more especially delight to make him the victim of their malicious sport; slyly fastening a rope around the neck of the unlucky sneak, they teaze him into bell-madness.

Reader, did you ever live in old London? If so, you will remember well a bell, that, accompanied by a husky cry of "Dust O!" aroused you often from your morning slumbers. It never did anything else but cry out for house sweepings; the very lowest, smallest trader among Bells Commercial, made, no doubt, out of bits of old refuse metal, fragments of German silver spoons, shreds of tin, headless pins and eyeless needles, missing buttons and discarded teapots,—the sifted gatherings of the cart. Alas, poor hack! born badly and brought up badly, never, we fear, did your dust-begrimed sides get a decent polish! This bell was put down some time ago.

Decidedly Disagreeable Bells—are there any? Let the schoolboy answer. Hear what he has to say about that "tin pot," as he calls it. Crabbed old cynic; he watches from his dingy shed for the exact and special time when the youngsters are in the very heat and rapture of their game, and pounces down upon them with an aggravating "All boys in!" Detestable dog in the manger! Would that we could

> "Bury thee certain fathoms in the earth,
> Or deeper than did ever plummet sound;"

drown thee, rope, dingy shed, and all! Yet, strange to say, as the manner of many bells is, this gruff boy-hater manages to change his tone somewhat as the hour of dismissal strikes its magic note; not but that the janitor has to bend to the pull before the surly fellow will give the sign.

The Curfew, when he acted the part of a huge extinguisher of the national fires and lights, must have been a most inconvenient and disagreeable meddler. Fancy yourself, good friend—it is well to make things personal—only just fancy yourself in the very act of grilling a kidney for supper, or boiling the water with reference to that "merest drop" you take for health's sake at close of day, when suddenly—there being no watch in the house, mind you, as neither Geneva levers nor American clocks existed in the days of the Conqueror—quite suddenly, the bell strikes out your fire in the tinkling of its tongue, out, out, right out into dead darkness, the kidney unturned upon the bars, and the water lukewarm in the pot! Fancy that, my patient friend, if you can, and say was not the Curfew a most unpleasant fellow? He is but a harmless ghost of a bell now, to be found haunting only the very oldest belfries in the very oldest towns, themselves little else but ghosts, while even there fires respect him not, the chimneys flouting him with their smoke long after eight of the clock.

The Porter's Bell, hard by park gates and grand court entrances, always seems to us to be gruff and grim—like the porter himself for that matter, and the porter's dog and the porter's wife; but we'll not insist on it; we may be mistaken now and then in our opinions of bell character, being liable to err and so forth with interpreters of higher pretensions. We had some thought of putting in the Factory Bell along with the disagreeables; in fact, we have a notion that it is something more than disagreeable,—hard, unfeeling, inclined to bear down heavily upon its duteous slaves, and rather prone to grind a little now and then in its sharp, peremptory motions. But doubtless that is another prejudice, so let it pass.

Pleasant bells, most pleasant, we take the liberty of thinking, are all they that tinkle and stop, stop and then tinkle, upon the necks of browsing cattle. Gathering sweetness from the flowers they bend towards, and catching song-sprinklings from the birds they send, but little startled, to the sky or bush, they glad the ear of the saunterer set free awhile from the buzz of towns. Bless thee, thou long-faced, stupid old bellwether! and thou, too, full-eyed, full-uddered leader of the dairy herd! We like thy music better by far than that of many city concerts we have heard. Pleasant, too, to meet—mind, only to meet in passing, not to sit behind—pleasant the Waggon Bells from the arched crest of the team; at least, they used to be so a long time ago, before the Railway Bell put them out, and made our highways silent. Likewise pleasant are Camel Bells, as we have heard them, dangling from the long necks

L

of Commissariat trains on Eastern roads, a long undulating line of sound, faint, then full, in waves of ebb and flow. But how much more pleasant must those bells sound to the hungry ears of the desert traveller weary with long silence! Let them be the most crooked, cracked abortion that ever flowed from furnace, yet must they send out heavenly music to his hearing; sign of another fate, another voice, to break the sameness of the everlasting sands.

But are there not also bells that are terrible? Fearful voices! Thank Heaven they are not often heard amongst us! Now and then, as the ages pass, some of them affright us with their sullen cries. Such was the Bell of the Plague, which day and night, in every street and lane of stricken London, tolled out the departed to the passing carts and the insatiable grave-pits. "Give out your dead!" it cried to the trembling inmates, themselves marked with the fatal spot. Horrid bell; mayest thou never more be heard in this world! There is yet another of this family. Listen!

> "Hear the loud Alarum Bells!
> Brazen bells!
> What a tale of terror now, their turbulency tells!
> In the startled ear of night,
> How they scream out their affright!
> Too much horrified to speak,
> They only shriek, shriek
> Out of time,
> In a clamorous appeal to the mercy of the fire,
> In a mad expostulation to the deaf and frantic fire,
> Leaping higher, higher,
> With a desperate desire.
> O, the bells, bells, bells!
> What a tale their terror tells
> Of despair!

> How they cleave, and clash, and roar!
> What a horror they outpour
> On the bosom of the palpitating air!"

So chimes the poet who knew all peals; this terrible one also.

Then there are certain bells that, if legends have any truth in them, possess a mystic charm. "Fairy Bells," we presume, are so endowed; but, as we never heard them ring, being no poet, we like not to be positive in our presumption. About the famous Bow Bells, however, we have less hesitation. Are they not uncanny? Are they not always associated in the general mind with Whittington, that mythical Lord Mayor? also with Whittington's cat, that fabulous mouser and obvious "familiar"? Moreover, do they not bewitch the organs of speech of all born within the reach of their sound, so that invariably and otherwise most unaccountably in the mouth of all true Cockneys the *v* and the *w* ring most confounding and perpetual changes?

What of the Incheape Bell? The bell that stood a warning beacon on an ocean rock, and which, hung round with a drapery of sea-weed, swung out ghostly peals as the wave rose and fell against the sides! How to the ears of superstitious mariners, keeping watch in the dead of the night, sounded the fitful tollings, mingling with the sighing and the howling of the gale among the shrouds? Bell of mystery! Bold indeed was the hand that unslung it from its holding and dropped it into the fathomless deep. Fearful were the sounds that gurgled up as it sunk, foretelling the fate of the foolhardy man, afterwards wrecked on the rock he had despoiled. Passed away is that bell. But another, for aught we know, still sends the sailor to his phantom stories, ringing down mystery from the clouds or stars. We tell the tale as we know it. As a ship went southward, keeping gallant course before the winds, she came into the region of huge sea-birds, and—

"At length did cross an albatross,"

which some weary passenger, who had, may be, left his wisdom on "the line," by some cunning angling caught, and, for lazy sport's sake, around its neck fastened a bell, then sent it off again to its air liberties. Tinkle, tinkle, tinkle, it went chiming over the waves; and over the waves it tinkles still, no doubt, for it is a long life they live that bathe in the sea. It is not every one who knows this story. Out of the thousands that sail on the deep, not a score, perhaps, have heard it told; and many as they pass along in the dusk and the dawn will turn their ear to the going and the coming of the Albatross Bell, wondering at the mystery.

Jubilant Bells!—they that strike our choral thunderings of triumph, keeping time and tune with a nation's joy, rivalling the booming of the guns, flinging challenges of sound to the reverberating clouds, sending buzzing pleasures down the belfries, to the quivering foundations, to the shaking earth! Bells of Victory! not unmingled with some sadness for the slain. Bells of Peace! sweet and gladsome as those bygone voices that out of heaven sang—

"On earth peace, and good will towards men."

Coronation Bells! outtelling proudly a people's loyalty and love. And then, too—perhaps the most rejoicing bell of all—the bell that tells through all the house the safe return of one long loved.

And now our changes are nearly all run out. Fittingly for the last we have reserved some Solemn Chimes. Solemn, yet not sullen, and not wholly solemn some of them. Church Bells, for instance, "the poetry of the steeples;" their Sabbath soundings seem half rejoicings, glad pæans of triumph over hard labour, painful earnings, anxious cares, and gross delights. They clear and soothe the air that has been vexed by the turmoil of the week, spreading out around its gentle atmospheres of rest and quiet thought, helping upward on their winged voices our sluggish prayers and hopes. Thus seem they full of joy and gentle assistance; yet are they solemn as become messengers that summon us to a worship that ever must commence with sorrowful confessions.

The Vesper Bell has given a theme to painter and poet. At one time no picture was more commonly exhibited in London art shop-windows than one in which a boat appeared on quiet waters, bearing a monk, a girl, and a ferryman;—the monk told his beads; the lifted oar dropped, and the girl listened meekly, while the bell sounded from the convent on the shore. It was a picture which needed no description. The poet said—

"——Blessed be the hour!
The time, the chime, the spot, where I so oft
Have felt that moment in its fullest power
Sink o'er the earth so beautiful and soft,

> While swung the deep bell in the distant tower,
>   Or the faint dying day hymn stole aloft,
> And not a breath crept through the rosy air,
>   And yet the forest leaves seemed stir'd with prayer.
> Soft hour! which makes the wish and melts the heart
>   Of those who sail the seas, on that first day
> When they from their sweet friends are torn apart;
>   Or fills with love the pilgrim on his way
> As the far bell of Vesper makes him start,
>   Seeming to weep the dying day's decay.
> Is this a fancy which our reason scorns?
> Ah! surely nothing dies but something mourns!"

And now we must own there is a bell whose mournful monotone has sad echoes in all hearts. Dread Monitor! With solemn voice vibrating through the minute pauses, he tells off another and another and another from the lists of life. The Passing Bell will be heard, and it were but sorry cowardice to attempt to silence him or to drop him from our list, but we may freely hope that Time will ring out many changes before his services are needed. Happily the merry bells are those which make the most noise and sound the most frequently.

TWO OLD BOOKS.

We have a friend who has taken the agreeable fancy to present us from time to time with sundry articles of curious interest. It is seldom he meets us without emptying his pockets and filling ours with choice specimens of something or other. Now it is the skull of a rare bird, picked up during a ramble on the sands; anon it is a section of an ant's nest, done up carefully in brown paper; then the thorny skin of a hedgehog, a rhinoceros beetle, or a cunning spider's den. Lately his benevolence has taken another shape; he has made it his delight to make us his depository of *recherché* literature, anticipating certain modest scruples on our part by assuring us that he got the rubbish at a sale for a mere song—that, moreover, the good wife did not like to see the things knocking about the house. A couple of weeks ago he handed over to us a bundle of antediluvian *London Gazettes*, very yellow, very musty, very blotchy, yet still in fine preservation. This gift was speedily followed up by a presentation of a copy of "Crabbe's Poems, first edition, folio," and two volumes of the "Companion to the Newspaper," brimful of political economy and reform statistics. Just about the time that the last underground extension was talked about, he met us smilingly in the street and placed in our accustomed hand one of the earliest pamphlets on locomotives, "supposing," as he said, "that it might be interesting just now." A few days back he surprised us, on turning a corner, with two ancient-looking tomes, which turned out on inspection to be "A Practical New Grammar with Exercises of Bad English, by A. Fisher," just a hundred years old; and "An Arithmetick, both Theory and Practice," still older by some thirty years, author's name not mentioned. We made our best bow for the handsome gift of "rubbish," took them home, discussed a few pages with our evening's tea and toast, and finding that they made us "laugh consumedly," we thought a few extracts might do the same kind office for our readers.

We will take the *Grammar* first, as in duty bound, inasmuch as Mr. Fisher tells us in his Preface that "Grammar is truly accounted the Basis of Literature, and the source from which all other sciences do proceed." A pretty tolerable amount of picking might be obtained from the Orthographical and Etymological heaps; but as rubbish is not the kind of article best suited to our readers, we will at once pass on to rake a little amongst the choice deposits of our author's Syntax and Prosody; and can scarcely do better than commence with the chapter on "Grammatical Figures."

Most people have doubtlessly some idea of a *Pleonasm;*

yet scarcely any will have chanced to light upon a definition at once so perspicuous and beautiful as the following: "A Pleonasm denotes Luxuriancy." Exactly so; it is the very oasis of figures, a tropical over-growth of language and letters,—that too muchness of a good thing so seldom realized. But now for the "examples," with which Mr. Fisher appropriately illustrates his happy and suggestive explanation. "The Pleonasm," says Mr. F., "occurs in such sentences as these: *I saw it with my eyes*, for *I saw it; * again, *as yet*, for *yet;* again, *Ann and Mary and Sarah and Jane*, for Ann, Mary, Sarah, and Jane." Here indeed is "Luxuriancy!" Instances these are of a profuse squandering of precious words, that may well make us deem Jeremy Taylor parsimonious and Macaulay rather shabby than otherwise. But let this "figure" give way to another. "What," demands Mr. F., "is an *Enallage?*" On coming to this question we drank a preliminary cup of tea, had in the candles, called in the nut-crackers and looked out E in Walker. Not, however, obtaining perfect satisfaction, we resorted to Mr. Fisher, and to our surprise we found that our landlady had produced an Enallage when she laboriously wrote out, and painfully wafered up in the window, the notice that attracted our attention to our present quarters —"A House to Let *i*nquire within,"—enquire would have been a simple propriety, but that unlucky substitution of an *i* for an *e* made an Enallage of it beyond hope. This example at once satisfied us, and we sent the nut-crackers back in disgrace, and put Walker on the shelf upside down, and undusted, as a mark of our displeasure. And now, reader, to what figure of speech do you fancy the following select sentences belong? "He drank it all up, and gave away the rest." "My master, his son, and I were alone in the garden." "The house is full of people before anybody comes in." To us they seem rather stupid specimens of the Hibernian Bull or British Blunder. Mr. Fisher, however, glorifies them under the high and lofty title of *Solecisms*.

Dinner parties are occasionally rather dull affairs; probably, therefore, the following "*Witticisms, or Simple Conceits*," will be an acceptable contribution to the table-talk of the day. "'Tis true as truth itself." "He was hampered in Hampshire." "Though she is fair, she is rare." "A jockey being asked the age of a horse, clapped his hands upon the back of the beast and affirmed he was under five, meaning his four fingers and thumb." "He remembered all he did not forget." Yet these smart things, admirable as they may be, are nothing to "*Complex Conceits*." These, especially the Ænigma, abound with equivocations, metaphors, subtle representations, seeming contradictions, etc., and being enveloped as it were within themselves, or as a wheel within a wheel, require great strength of thought and reason to solve many of them; as a person being asked his name, answered *twenty shillings;* meaning *Mark* (*i.e.*, 13*s*. 4*d*.) *Noble* (6*s*. 8*d*.) which, together, make twenty shillings. Or if one should say of yesterday—

"I was to-morrow, but am not to-day,
Yet shall by two days hence, my name display."

The good citizen, in the French play, was made happy with astonishment at his own learning when he discovered that he had been talking prose all his days. How much more delighted were we to find from Mr. Fisher that we had been in the constant habit of using in the most familiar manner, in our common speech, the *Synecdoche*, the *Catachresis*, the *Autonomasia*, the *Antimetaloble*, the *Paralepsis*, and the *Diasyrmus*. "Synecdoche," says our author, "implies the whole by a part, or a part by the whole; as, he is an honest soul (*i.e.*, man); a bright genius (*i.e.*, man); this is a bottom (*i.e.*, ship)." Again: "A Catachresis borrows the name of one thing to express another, as, To hold (*i.e.*, to lay) a wager. To make (*i.e.*, to teach) a dog."

But we must now glean a little in another field. The deeply artful manner in which the following specimens of bad English are constructed so as to puzzle the student, is inimitable. "Your father is very healthy, though she be turned of sixty." "Lauk! what a great flock of geese is there, where is they fed?" "Thou art the most wisest boy I ever saw." The excellent Mrs. Partington very likely learnt her extraordinary peculiarities of phonetic spelling from Mr. Fisher's "bad orthography." Our readers will thank us for the following piece of advice, rendered all the more impressive by its picturesque garb. We quote it from "*Rules for Polite and Useful Conversation:*"—"He that is polleit, will in course obsarve to conform hisself to the taste, carrector, and preasant youmour of his company, but this is never found where the parson does not first endeavour to stock hisself with a large fund of good natir and complesence, but as he nevir succeads that forces natir, I do not pretend to say, that any rasional parson ought to balk his talent in conversation, on the contrarey, never attempt ralarey or a youmerous storey if your tallant is not for youmer or ralarey. Consider your capacitie, and keep within the bounds of what you know. Never talk of things you are ignorant of, unless it be for information." Mr. Fisher was too polite a soul (excuse the Synecdoche), to forget the ladies, so he has devoted an entire chapter to "Maxims for the Fair Sex." Now the maxims being taken from the *Spectator*, are undeniably sage, but being adorned in Mr. F.'s bad, bad English, they look most unmistakably ridiculous; as witness this choice quotation:—"When Addam is enterduced by Milton describing Eve in Paradice, and relating to the angel the impressions he felt upon seeing her at her first creation, he does not represent her as a Grecian Venus, by her shape and features, but by the lustre of her mind which shoon in them and gave them their pour of charmin,—

> Grace was in all her steps, heven in her ey,
> In all her gesters dignety and love!

without this iradiatin poor, the proudest fair one ought to now, whatever hir glace may tell hir to the contrary that hir most perfect features are uninformed und ded. I cannot betor close this morel than by a short epitaph written by Ben Johnson, with a spirit which nothing cud inspire but such an object as I have been describing,—

> Unde nith this stone doth lie
> As much virtu as cud die,
> Which when alive did vigor give
> To as much buity as cud live."

There are few things more difficult than to read poetry with even tolerable correctness; a direction or two from our learned grammarian will not therefore be deemed the "drop too much." Mr. Fisher's great and golden rule for reading verse is "to pronounce every word and every sentence just as if it were prose, observing the stops, placing the accent on a particular sylable in a word, and a just emphasis on a word or words in a sentence." Excellent well, no doubt, Mr. F.; but for ourselves we may say that our difficulty has always been just that of the cook who had to catch the hare as a preliminary to skinning. We have always felt convinced that we ought to accent the right syllables, and emphasize the right word; but for the life of us we could never find the one or the other. One thing, however, will trouble us no longer—we shall know in future what to do with intractable rhymes. "How to favour the rhyme is to pronounce the last word of the line so as to make it chime with the line foregoing, where the word admits of two pronunciations, as—

> If I was once from Bondage free
> I'd never sell my Liberty.

Here you are to pronounce the word *Liberty* as if it were written with *ee*,—Libertee—that it may rhyme with the word *free*. But if the verse runs thus:—

> My soul ascends above the Sky,
> And triumphs in her Liberty,

Then the word *Liberty* is to be sounded as ending in *i*—Liberti—that sky may have a just rhyme to it." In concluding his remarks on this section of his work, Mr. F. gives a most admirable help to critics, which we intend to use. "If," says he, "the verse does not read well and harmonious to the ear, when it reads like prose, you are to charge the fault to the Poet, and not to the reader." Here truly is the grand art and secret of criticism! We shall have no further trouble with the poets. If they do not happen to trip off pretty smoothly from our tongue into our ear, they are no true children of the muse, but bantlings born of Synecdoches and Antimtalobles. We are afraid it is but a poor look-out for Browning, Tennyson, and other unfortunates, whom we shall never be able to read to our liking, let us be ever so prosaic.

There are several other tit-bits which we had marked for selection, but having another candidate for honours, we must allow the lore of Fisher to repose between its stout calf covers. Nor shall we, as it is, be able to do much for the glory of the "Arithmetick." Who the author of this treatise is we cannot positively say, the title-page of the book being lost. Nor does the preface, written by H. Ditton, of Christ's Hospital, help us in this matter, for although he refers to this Junius of Numbers, he does so under the mysterious style of "The author (whoever he was)." But as a little further down he tells us to "take him purely as an Arithmetician," perhaps we cannot do better than consider him to be an elder brother to Babbage's famous reckoning automaton. That our selections may be received with suitable reverence and gravity we will give the opinions of the Blue-coat Master, and also that of Mr.

Snell, "Schoolmaster, of Foster Lane." "It appears to me," we quote the former pedagogue, "upon the perusal of this book, to be a curious piece! 'Tis clean, methodical, and handsomely dressed: so plain, that the dullest person may learn by it, and so compleat, that he need learn no more." Mr. Snell (who is so conscientious an arithmetician that he divides his favours between the old and new style of dating, by writing the year fractionally after this fashion, —"March 7, 1720-21") says, sententiously,—" I have read this book; and finding it very well done, recommend it to such as desire a good knowledge of arithmetic." We cordially go along with both these gentlemen in their appreciation of the book; and that our readers may have the chance of uniting in this reciprocity, we favour them with the following "Example of Geometrical Progression," begging them to observe particularly the sort of young man who figures as chief personage in the transaction:—A Merchant having a soft young Man to his Son, covetous enough, but scarce able to keep a Shop-Book, was minded to purchase for him some considerable Lands in the Country; and bid him enquire out some handsome Estate that would be sold, and he would buy it for him. The young Man, overjoyed at the News, runs to an Inn, where he heard diverse Country-Gentlemen lodg'd; and in all haste ask'd them if any of them would sell their Estate; most of them were very angry, and near beating of him; but one of them being a facetious Gentleman, resolv'd to put a Trik upon him; and told him, That he had a Neat Hall with a goodly Park and Manor, on the Bank of a

Pleasant River, and a great Number of sufficient Tenants; all of which, with the Royalty of a fair Market Town, and the Patronage of a Parish Church, belonging thereto, should be his, upon Condition he would lay him down one Penny on the Threshold of the Porch-Door belonging to the Hall, Two-pence at the Next Door, Four-Pence at the 3rd Door, and so on doubling, 'till he had gone thro' all the Doors, which were 54 in all. 'I'll have it,' saith the young Man, 'and here's a Piece in Earnest;' and in all haste tells his Father what a Purchase he had made, wishing him to give him an Hundred Pounds, for that he thought could not but abundantly satisfy. 'Thou Calf,' quoth the Father, 'the King of *Spain's* Revenues would not pay what thou hast promised, if they were sold at 20 Years Value, much less can my Estate pay for thy Purchase, for it will not bring thee past the 24th Threshold. The best is, the Gentleman knows thee not; and if he did, he could get no Advantage of one that has nought; but I'll warrant thee, he is making merry with a Fool's earnest. Now I desire to know what the sum to be laid down on the 24th Threshold was, and what the Whole, which he promised would have come to?' *First.*—The Sum to be laid down on the 24th Threshold, by *Proposition* 1, will be found to be 8388608 Pence. And by this *Proposition* the sum of the whole unto the 24th Threshold will be found to be 16777215 Pence, equal to £66905 1s. 3d. which the Father must be worth, else he could not bring him over the 24th Threshold. *Secondly.*—The Number to be laid down on the 64th Threshold, by the said first *Proposition*, 9223372036854775808 Pence; and by this *Proposition* the Sum of the Whole, which the young Man should have given for the Purchase, will be 18440744073709551615 Pence, equal to 76861433610456465 Pounds, 1 Shilling and 3 Pence; by which it may appear the Gentleman spoke within Compass; For this Sum would Purchase the yearly Rent of £38430716820 22823 5s. 0d. ¾, which is a great deal more than the King of *Spain's* Revenues are worth; For supposing his Revenues are worth One Hundred Millions *per Ann.* (which I think no Potentate of the Earth is worth) it would be no more considerable to the Sum last mentioned, than a Red-Herring of an Ounce Weight would be to the loading of 20 Ships of 50 Tons Burden a-piece, which may be thus demonstrated; for allowing 20 Hundred to the Ton, the whole number of Ounces, equal to the burthen of so many Ships of such Capacity, will be 35840000; and this Number of Ounces multiplied by One Hundred Million, is only 3584000000000000, which is less than the aforegoing Number by 259071682022823, which is a Number large enough to load a great many more ships." This *exposé* of the "soft young man's" covetousness and folly is so lengthy, that we have only space enough left for the subjoined problem, the solution of which may probably give our readers a little pleasant occupation during the long evenings of the winter. "A Gentleman having a Coat and Waste-coat with 12 Dozen of Silver Buttons: A Baker seeing it, demands of the Gentleman the Price thereof;

who answered, If he would double every Button with a Barley-Corn, proceeding from the first gradually to the last, it should be his. To which the Baker assents. 'I,' says the peremptory arithmetician, 'demand the Number of Barley-Corns, together with the Worth and Weight of the same.'"

AN AMATEUR.

More than twenty years ago there lived in a lovely "suburban residence" in the neighbourhood of a Devonshire town a young gentleman called David Bowes. His father died not long after David's birth, and his mother came into the property, including David, who was reckoned in the household inventory as an animated chattel. Early in life he was inaugurated with very little ceremony into the position of special underling in all the domestic departments: in the kitchen he was a scullion; suffusedly, throughout the house, a maid of all work; on the road to market or shop, an errand boy; on occasions of ceremonious tea-parties, a dumb waiter; on other occasions of ceremonious visitings, a carrier of clogs and umbrella. Thus he grew up to man's estate under a dreadful tyranny and stultification; the maternal apron-strings upon his hands, chains about his legs, a collar round his neck, and a gag in his mouth.

Is it to be wondered at that, under these decidedly depressing circumstances, there should be a deformed and proportionate outgrowth somewhere? that David Bowes bulged in domestically, should bulge out conspicuously in some other direction? And, considering that his organ of constructiveness was rather large, considering also that a box of tools was amongst the odds and ends of his inheritance, is it to be wondered at that the tendency of his particular bulge should be towards mechanics? Whether this be the philosophy of the case or not, David Bowes became an amateur-mechanic. Seizing and diligently using every stray second, fragment, and fag-end of time, he notched, whittled, sawed, nailed, tacked, glued, bored, screwed, braced and bitted, dovetailed, spoked, gouged, punched, fitted in and fitted up, from downy boyhood to the time when he chiselled off the bristles from his manly face. Happily the world yielded planks! Happily for him, loosened for a moment from the apron-string he could take shelter in a rabbit-box, a dove-cote, or a dog-kennel, or, launching into a washing-tub a miniature bark, could sail forth upon that sea far out of sight of kitchen, shop-errand, umbrella, and slave-holding mamma. As our genius grew older he became more ambitious, and employed the cunning of his hand on certain serious labours.

His first great work was a Back Door. Well do we remember the premonitory noises peculiar to carpentry that for some weeks preceded the finishing strokes; well also the portentous face of David, every feature big with the coming triumph; well also the door itself as it shone forth upon us in the lustre of its first appearance. The amateur had risen early to his labour, and just as we threw open our bedroom window to the morning, there he was standing off at a little distance, admiring his handiwork with the zeal of an inventor. Most decidedly his feelings that moment were those of a discoverer,—the maker of a new thing. If you fancy that that Back Door was like back doors in general, that only shows your ignorance of amateurs. These gentlemen, let them try their hand at what they please, whether it be Acts of Parliament, cutting bread and butter, or laying out a garden walk, do what they do always with a difference. The ordinary back door is the same all the world over; everybody knows that it consists of a certain number of plain upright planks, nailed on to a certain number of rather heavy cross pieces, the whole set up in a plain honest frame, painted for the most part lead colour, and fitted up with a thumb latch and a couple of antiburglarious bolts. That we take to be the back door of common life. But David's Back Door was, you may believe, another sort of thing. It was planned and executed to meet the peculiar exigencies of his back door life. It must be told that there was another bond slave in the household besides our friend; there was a hen, a solitary hen, held in duty bound to lay an egg daily for the great owner's breakfast, and in default thereof to be twisted in the neck, plucked, and roasted for the great owner's dinner, another victim being duly bought and bound to lay. Now as this hen in the course of duty had to go out and pick up materials for the demanded egg, David cut a hole in the bottom of his door by way of accommodation for his fellow-servant, and, being tasty, shaped it gothically. Fowl holes however, we confess are common enough in the commonest back doors. But observe! the great owner held in bondage also a pet dog, a slave to daily washings and combings; hence another gothic hole was cut for the dog; and a similar one for a captive cat. Should it be asked—why? why could not one opening do for the three? we can only remind the reader David Bowes was an amateur. The Back Door is beginning to be somewhat peculiar. Still there were other exigencies—requiring adaptations. David was nervously sensitive and highly bashful. Doomed by his inexorable mother to take in the milk, he couldn't bear to face the milk-maid; and so he made another hole half-way up the door, through which he put out his jug, had it filled, paid his penny, and retired without an interview! Again, —a very terrible and exacting exigency,—it was his lot, maugre his sensitiveness, to convey away and eject forth the household sloppery; for many a year he had endured the torturing shame of carrying the pail out into the back thoroughfare, and had been caught some and sundry times, burnt into his memory by his blushes, absolutely caught by certain eyes he wished to look his best in. This was to be no longer. Through another hole, still gothic, a nicely fitted movable spout, projecting as occasion might require to the kennel, the daily tribute was henceforth to flow from an unseen hand. And then, partly to serve the purposes of a letter box, partly to keep up the uniformity and have three holes above as well as three below, partly, perhaps mainly, because he was an amateur, he opened out a sixth and final hole likewise gothic, making altogether a unique and special back door, worthy, we hope, of this humble record.

The next great work was a Garden Gate. Now the back door was a thing of use, a necessary of every-day life, a drudge to be swung to and fro in the outgoings and incomings of work; anybody might rap at the back door, a dustman or a beggar; and, consequently, of course, excepting the gothic lavished on the holes, it was but a common piece of joinery after all; but the Garden Gate! that was for ornament, for the outward beauty, honour, and glory of the Bowes's abode, and would be confronted by visitors of ceremony and state. Accordingly David, previously to entering upon this work, gave himself up to the study of the true and the beautiful in architectural entrances. Gateways, ancient and modern, Athenian porticoes, Roman triumphal arches, Druidic rectangles, and Mediæval porches were all severally and comparatively considered with a view to the right and fitting style of thing for the gate of his garden. The result was a couple of pillars, only to be described as being very composite indeed, and a door of many panels, each panel separate and distinct in form and painted of a different colour; a frame of flaming crimson toning down and harmonizing the whole. As a work of art the entrance was finished, but not so as a conventional garden gate to a respectable suburban residence. Where was the brass plate? where the bells? Restless after perfection, David began to bulge out more mechanically than ever, nay, more artistically. He obtained a graver, practised letter-cutting, and in a few months had the lofty satisfaction of screwing on a foot square of brass with BOWES, in very large eccentric and ornate capitals, in the centre, and *Bowes sculp.* in small italics in the corner. What a time that was for the boys! Every little urchin passing by catching sight of the blaze, made "Bowes!" a street call for a week. David felt rather uncomfortable. The publicity was rather more than he expected; it interfered with his digestion, and for several nights he went in troubled dreams through the various processes involved in screwing on the plate to his back, unscrewing it, and swallowing it to escape notoriety. As the novelty wore off, and the boys found a new cry, David recovered his complacency—in fact, used the gate twice as often as he had done before. Still there were no bells. The amateur was vexed to hear the complaints of visitors over their abused knuckles sore and red with continuous knocking on one of the many-coloured panels. On one occasion, just after the piece of architecture was put up, an old lady, of vigorous passions, astonished the unfortunate porter (always David) immediately the gate was opened, by thrusting in his face a straw-coloured glove bedaubed with vermilion, the hue of the particular panel she had been attacking, unmindful of the paint. We believe, in fact, that the glove went so near David's face, as to leave a brilliant blush upon the tip of his nose. Under torture of various mortifications David bulged out into a bell-hanger, and within three weeks of the accident there appeared imbedded in the gate post, three bell handles, over which appeared severally the inscriptions, "Visitor's Bell," "Servant's Bell," and "Night

Bell." Suitably to the department allotted to each bell, the visitor's handle was delicate in size and made of some fancy wood, just the very thing for dainty begloved hands; the servant's handle was stout and strong; while the handle of the night bell was a big bulb of iron pendant from an iron rod, and evidently connected with a most tremendous terrifier at the household end. If the question should be asked, "Why three bells?" we may for our part say that's the very question we ourselves put at the time. Why, O David, a servant's bell, seeing that you were the only domestic in that mansion? Yet perhaps for this one there was a reason. The difference in the peals enabled David probably to decide whether he might rush off to dishabille from sloppery or carpentry, or whether he had better make himself presentable. But the night bell! What could he want of that? He was neither a surgeon, a monthly nurse, nor a night man; then why the night bell? We never heard that David gave any reason for this anomaly, and we surmise that it must be ranked along with the sixth hole in the back door, an outgrowth of David's amateurship. But what a grand public benefit did all boydom find in those three bells! What changes were rung upon them! How many times had the unlucky inventor to run a bootless errand to the gate! What a nuisance did the ever tinkling three become to the whole neighbourhood! At last, to release himself from duty, and for the quiet of the neighbourhood, David detached the wires from the handles, thus securing peace without sacrificing appearances.

Resting awhile after the achievements and disappointments of the great garden labour, David gave up his leisure to visions and reveries; at least, so it is supposed by his friends, for the next great work that issued from his hands was a summer house. There was a strip of ground in front of the residence: it had a south-eastern aspect, and was flooded from a little after dawn with the morning and noon sunshine. To this David, in the hot and glaring summer weather, had a natural objection, and was determined to soften, tone down, if not altogether do away with the unpleasantness, by erecting a bower of considerable relative dimensions. Accordingly, on the principle of attacking the enemy in his stronghold, David selected for the site of his summer house the upper and sunniest section of the garden strip. There would he build up a defence against the solar rays. And he did it, too, bulging out for the occasion into a glass-painter and builder; for, although the Crystal Palace was not in existence in these days, our amateur was determined to use glass, as in his opinion the most suitable material. In after times, when the Exhibition was making a show-year of 1851, he, in his own private view, considered Paxton a copyist of himself. Furthermore, considering that simple glass in itself is scarcely a moderator of heat and light, he decided on dipping the raw material in tasteful dyes of deep and positive hues. We have forborne to say anything about David's personal appearance, and we only refer to it now by way of accounting for the particular colours selected by David for his bower. His hair was red, and he did not like it, as in his time it had not been discovered that the colour under another name was a peculiar beauty. His face was ruddy, like his hair, and this troubled him also, for he was vain. Hence he selected yellow and crimson for his glass, deciding that no one should have the advantage of him in the Bower; everybody there would be red alike then; and thus at least, if not liberty, equality and fraternity would find an appropriate temple in his garden! With David, to design was to accomplish. Speedily the growing fabric uprose. David strutted about within his summer house, a huge flaring bird of paradise. There he bathed himself in the tinted glory, there he basked himself in the metamorphosed rays, there he received all visitors, there he indemnified himself in golden-draperied dreams for the sad realities of sloppery, errandry, and all sorts and conditions of drudgery in general. Yet, it may strike you, as it did ourselves and others at the time, that as a means of moderating the effects of light and heat, that is to say for the purposes for which the summer house was built, fiery and flashy hues could not be the most appropriate. In fact, it was generally observed by all favoured visitors that they issued from the bower with a sense of having been half baked, feeling decidedly dry and crisp about the skin. But doubtlessly the amateur knew best. He was satisfied. He had beaten the sun—"done him," if not "brown," quite red and crimson, and secured full half of his garden to his private personal pride and pleasure.

David's next great work was an Organ. Concerning this, however, we have but little to say, as we never entered the interior of David's residence; very possibly had we done so, we might have had other and worthier deeds to chronicle. We were acquainted with the fact that David now and then bulged out a little as a convivialist in small tea-parties; we had also heard that the great maternal owner prided herself on her slave's accomplishments in this way, and had duly threatened him, notwithstanding his manhood, with "the corner," on occasions when David's modesty assumed the form of a violent cold. True also, about the period in question, we heard from time to time, issuing from the general apertures of the house, the holes in the back door included, sundry strange grumblings, howlings, and peculiar jerky, complaining squeakings, which we, it must be told to our disgrace, took to be David's bills of remonstrances, grievances, and petitions of relief presented to his harsh legislative and executive mamma. True also, we had detected "tune" strongly developed towards the outer angles of David's eye. Yet for all this we had not suspected the Organ. We never took the trouble to inquire into the peculiarities of its make; all the inkling we got about it was that David had built it in the bower; where, seated amidst the blazing effulgence of painted sunlight, letting loose, now sighing, now stormy melody with his rosy finger tips, he looked the very apotheosis of amateurs.

About the period at which we have now arrived, David was released from slavery by the hand of the greatest of all abolitionists. Inheriting himself together with the other "properties," he did as he listed, and amongst other things began to alter the premises in the back yard. Knowing that it was the usual practice for new inheritors to remodel, or extend their ancestral residence,—sending the front to the rear and the rear to the front, converting the Elizabethan into the Romanesque, adding on a wing or widening out a staircase,—we paid but little attention to David's dabbling in brick and mortar. As, however, the alteration gradually became completed, we began to be somewhat anxious. There was the look of a stable about the improvement. A large double door opened out immediately into the back lane—a big double door, with ventilator above—evidently a stable. We became sad and began to moralize; here, thought we, is another case of the everlasting sort, youthful impetuosities, kept in under double parental pressure, suddenly, on removal of that pressure, bursting forth into vigorous and wild waste;—here is this David, miserable drudge, harmless amateur, about to run to ruin on horseback. Various venerable ladies, ancient ceremonious visitors of the mamma, sympathized with us in our lamentations, lifted up their eyes, and set themselves on the general look-out for David's follies, more especially for the horse. But neither they nor any one else could get a glimpse of his tail. It was a matter of general remark in the neighbourhood that "David's horse had not come yet." It was of no use for the old ladies to sniff as they passed the stable door; of no use was it for the boys to climb up and peep through the ventilator; neither the smell nor the sight of a steed could be detected. Rumour, you may be sure, was alive;

"Mr. B." (he was Mr. B. now) "intended to wait till the races;" or, "the Sultan had sent a present of some Arabs to her Majesty, more than her Majesty wanted, and Mr. B. was waiting for the auction;" or, "Mr. B. had his eye on the piebald in the circus, or the intelligent pony." David himself looked portentous and a little nervous, and this was put down as proof positive of his jockey intentions; for never does a man appear so uneasy and generally anxious as when he is about to buy a horse, with the thousand possible faults of jibbing, shying, backing, bolting, biting, bucking, spavin, grease, sprain, and all the other vices of pace, temper, wind, and limb, horse flesh is heir to. One morning it became evident from sundry marks of preparation going on about the residence that something was to take place, and of course that something was the horse. Accordingly, summoned by the electric agency of gossip, the neighbourhood yielded up its secret police, self-appointed detectives, Paul Prys, and innumerable boys, who gathered to the spot; the old ladies, whose windows opened on the scene, being at their post of observation. We ourselves, by a curious coincidence, happened to be walking up the lane, when "sesame!" open came the stable door, and sure enough out came David, mounted on the hitherto invisible steed. No Arab certainly, no piebald, no intelligent circus pony, but a sparkling, brilliantly painted, trimly built Velocipede, all of his own making. For some time it was rather difficult for the gallant rider to get his correct balance; then the starting was another difficulty, and the exertions of the gallant rider in overcoming these difficulties were evidently painful to himself, though they appeared to be rather agreeable than otherwise to the unsympathizing mob. On the first move the noble steed seemed inclined to back into the stable, then it rushed forth straight against the wall on the other side of the way; at last, with the assistance of a friend who pointed the head of the restive animal down the lane, and with the kindly help of another friend who gave the spirited beast a push behind, David went off through an admiring avenue of spectators, a triumphant, self-propelling amateur.

INSIDE "THE BANK."

It would puzzle the most imaginative and ingenious of descriptive writers to invest the outside of the Bank of England, as an architectural object, with any interest. The windowless, dwarfed, grimy, and unadorned walls, and the innumerable iron rails, present a hideous plainness to the eye to which Newgate itself is a relief. The entrances, which alone break the dismal monotony of inartistically arranged stones, are without grandeur. The graces have been sacrificed to security. The spaces where windows were, or should be, are built in and give a look of blank blindness to the whole building. Thieves might break in through glass, and so glass is discarded. The immense area within the horrid square would give a splendid breadth of base for a towering pile which in its mere massiveness would be majestic. But many stories add to the dangers from fire, and so the squat heap spreads itself out with a grovelling stuntedness. Although this building is the chief symbol of two of the greatest, if not the very greatest, forces in the world, money and credit, it is outwardly remarkable only for its meanness. To the eye it offers nothing but a sombre dulness, which is all the more oppressive when it is known that it encloses not only the accounts of the National Debt, but a grave-yard. It is, we presume, impossible to bring the Bank under the operations of the Artisans' Dwellings Bill, but it would undoubtedly be a relief to Mr. Peabody, who sits in his cushionless chair hard by, could he have something more cheerful to look at on his right than the unadorned ugliness of the Bank sides.

But once enter the gate and pass under the eye of the terrible Bank porter in the overwhelming cocked hat, which might serve for the roof of any ordinary detached villa, and an intense interest is at once awakened. Not that the interior arrangements at all contribute to produce this effect. With the exception of the grand Board Room, smallness and meagreness characterize the building right through. Some of the apartments are decidedly pokey. Not one of the offices is to be compared with the imposing halls of some of the joint-stock banks of the City. In many rooms the ceiling hangs low like a November sky, and adds a sense of oppression to the chastened feelings of the visitor. The corridors are like tunnels, the courts are scant, the staircases are narrow and crooked, and the vaults are merely cellars. The inner quadrangle is a garden—that is to say, some imprisoned trees and shrubs strive to bring forth leaves in spring and summer, which, however, in their speckled paleness and feeble flimsiness, look more like the ghosts of the vaulted notes than the fresh produce of living sap. A fountain sends out a play of water in the shape, and pretty much the size, of an inverted washing-basin. As a building the interior answers admirably to the exterior, and if it could be supposed that the object of filling up the windows was to prevent any one from seeing the inside, it would be impossible to quarrel with the arrangement. But the architectural defects are forgotten in the presence of that which the ungainly casket holds—money! not in the narrow, shallow streams that run in the hidden channels of circulation, but accumulated in a great central reservoir. Millions are here and there, on the right and the left, below, beneath. Gold, silver, and paper are the commodities of the place. The carts in the courts are laden with bars and blocks of the precious metals. The huge porter tugs at a truck which carries parcels of dollars wrapped in folds of sheepskin. You see hundreds of junior clerks counting banknotes faster than you could turn the leaves of a book. Here is a room, the walls of which are covered with boxes, and in each box is a revenue for a kingdom. Out of one box is taken a single parcel of notes of the exchangeable value of a million. You take it in your hand and every finger-tip balances its hundreds of thousands. In this department sovereigns are broken into bits as if they were buttons in a mangle. In that, a sheet of paper with the clink of a machine becomes a warrant of authority before which mind, soul, and body bow with submissive service. Here beats the heart of the world-wide commerce of to-day, and here also lies all that remains of that awful debt which, though dead, yet lives in taxes and dividends. It is from the central room of this place that the Bank rate issues, ruling the price of money, and making or marring fortunes by the multitude. Facts like these banish the windowless walls, the dwarfed stature, and even the cocked hat of the porter, from the deeply impressed mind. Probably no man entered the Bank of England for the first time without a consciousness of awe far deeper than anything produced by cathedral or court of justice. The first inclination is to remove the hat and reverentially look into it; but this thought is checked and rebuked by the conviction that no outward act or symbol of solemnity could be anything but mockery of that abasement of spirit which is fitting within the shrine of money. And to this humbleness of mind is added the tremor of fear when the visitor is informed that "the men in the recesses within the gate are detectives whose duty it is to look well to every new comer." In spite of the firmest conviction of personal honesty, an uncomfortable suspicion of possible accident or failure of virtue agitates the nerves. It is a singular fact that the moment a stranger passes the gates of the Bank and comes under the eye of the detectives, he looks like a criminal who is anxious to appear innocent. He is afraid to put his hands in his pocket or to take them out; and if, in a moment of forgetfulness, he happens to rattle his pence, he becomes abject in his endeavours to look as if he had not done it. Interesting as an hour in the Bank is, it is impossible to leave without a sigh of relief, and it is absolutely necessary to resort at once to

Pimm's for the refreshment which probably is best to be found in oysters, porter, and brown bread.

Not the least interesting room in the Bank is that in which the sovereigns sent in by the outside banks are weighed and tested. A pound must be a pound, or the Bank will have the difference. The scales to which the coins are submitted for trial are not only delicate, but prompt and summary; they not only detect and declare deficiency, but they execute justice, and hand over the guilty to be broken to pieces. A row of sovereigns, perhaps a hundred in number, slide slowly down a tube, open on the upper side, to a hole in a small table, through which, one by one, they fall upon a little horizontal disc which is the scale. This disc is supported and moved by the most sensitive machinery. In an instant, at the mere touch of the coin, it is weighed, and if of the required measure, it slips to the right into a metal box, and has the reward of the good in going straight to the Bank coffers for the happiness of re-issue and use, but if short by the fraction of a feather, the cunning and unerring disc turns to the left, and the dishonoured bit of metal—for it is then no more than that —is dropped into another box and is hurried away to the executioner hard by, who crushes and defaces it as a preliminary to the fires of the melter. A sharp account is kept of the coin from each bank, and a charge is made for each case of underweight, amounting on the average to about threepence in the pound. While we looked on, in the space of perhaps five minutes, several instances of criminal deficiency occurred, and we found the breaking and defacing machine busily at work. It is indeed a sad sight to witness the bruising and smashing of a beautiful pound sterling, and the marring of her Majesty's image, and the best feelings of human nature prompt to a rescue; but the Bank gloats over its victims, and the man who attempted to snatch a bad sovereign from its doom would be handed without mercy over to the Lord Mayor.

In another room the returned notes are examined, arranged, and bundled. On entering we were told that about £70,000 worth of paper had come in that morning and was being counted. Several scores of young fellows, safely fenced off by a screen, the upper panels of which are of glass, were busily engaged in clutching at heaps of notes —fives, tens, twenties, hundreds—subduing them to order, dipping finger and thumb into water, rustling over the crisp leaves, noting down dates and numbers, and squaring quantities into packages. Not a note which comes in is ever re-issued. Once passed over the counter it has seen its day and done its work. It is no longer a drop in the life-blood of commerce, but a dead thing to be buried away in the catacombs beneath, where it lies for seven years coffined in a box, and at the end of the seventh year it is burnt. We went down into the vaults—" the catacombs," as they are called by the wags of the Bank,—a musty, dark, intricate, noiseless, mysterious labyrinth, through which we had to grope with the help of lanterns that were not too brilliant. The passages are narrow gangways between blocks of iron shelves, on which are placed innumerable boxes, a foot square,—each box branded with letters and numbers, and each containing closely packed corpses that once were full of the life and power of a legal tender. It was a curious thought to think that thick around lay shrivelled bits of paper which, in their day above ground, were good for corn and oil and wine, use and pleasure, picture and book, travel and good hostelry, service and love. And yet in such a place, and amidst those surroundings, our guide, one of the chiefs of departments, was bound to have his joke. "It was customary," he said, "to startle the ladies, if there were any in company, and take toll. This was the Bank's little way in the catacombs." As if it were possible to steal a kiss in a grave! Before leaving the shades we received a printed form containing the following information:—"Bank of England, 1874. The stock of Paid notes for seven years is about 94,000,000 in number, and they fill 18,000 boxes, which, if placed side by side, would reach three miles. The notes placed in a pile would be eight miles high, or, if joined end to end, would form a ribbon 15,000 miles long; their superficial extent is more than that of Hyde Park, their original value was over £3,000,000,000, and their weight over 112 tons." This is an overwhelming statement, and yet it is not exhaustive. It is quite possible to let the imagination play other tricks with those quantities. That ribbon of notes would be long enough to fasten the North Pole to the South and leave considerable streamers at both ends. The superficial extent would be equal to the paper-hanging of half the houses in London. It would be death to the most adventerous climber to attack that paper "pile," to reach which Dhawalagiri might be heaped on Chimburazo and that on Kilmangaro in vain. The boxes themselves would make a front and back staircase to the loftiest peak of the Himalayas, or suffice for the next new palace for the Sultan, to whom probably it would give a new pleasure, could he build himself a seraglio and a divan out of cases of Bank of England notes.

The room full of virgin notes, ready for issue, is a charming place for the cultivation of self-denial. It is wainscoted with panels, each of which is a door double locked, and behind each door, as in a large pigeon-hole, lie piles of precious paper, which, as yet, no man has touched for use or profit. One of the doors is opened and a glimpse is had of wonderful possibilities of wealth in packets so compact that a million can be held in the hand. The officer in charge takes out a bundle and places it on the trembling palm of the visitor, who laughs childishly as he poises the paper thousands, and sighs to think he cannot clutch what he holds. The room full of sovereigns, boxed and bagged, is also a trying place. It was especially so to the man to whom the offer was made—so goes the Bank story—to take away with him a hatful of guineas provided he could carry it off by the brim. But after all the proposal was perfectly safe, as no brim could bear the weight. A trial would rend away the crown, and scatter the guineas upon the floor. It is also said that when the Shah—that monarch of singular manners—was in the Bank, it was necessary to avoid placing anything in his hands that he could carry, as he would be pretty certain to treat it as a gift. The bullion vaults are beautiful in the simplicity of their contents. Bars of gold and silver excite the imagination, but they present but little to the eye. The spoil from Coomassie in a glass case is more curious. The Ashantee trinkets, golden ornaments, rude in workmanship, but not without some elegance in design, have their associations. King Koffee and his wives wore them, and it is strange, not to say grotesque, to be reminded of a negro king while on a tour through the Bank of England.

Perhaps the printing department of the Bank is as intelligently interesting as any part of the institution. The mechanical creation of the note is there to be seen in all its processes. The blank paper—blank, but cleverly made and watered in secret ways, and ready to be converted into notes of any value—is held out to the eye, not to the hand, as visitors are requested "not to touch." The printing-machines employed, with their self-acting registers, and the Brahama invention for numbering, are beautiful specimens of dexterously applied means to cunningly devised ends. But printing is pretty much the same whether a thousand-pound note has to be struck off or a halfpenny newspaper.

The Bank has its curiosity shop and chamber of horrors, in which forgeries, monstrosities, and singularities are carefully preserved. Amongst the forgeries is one most adroitly made by a French prisoner of war—quite a feat of penmanship—and another by a Hindoo who managed to turn a ten-rupee note into one for a thousand. There is shown, with an air of triumph, a china inkstand, on the cover of which is stamped and glazed the image of a five-pound note; and an immense pocket-handkerchief is unfolded, literally covered with Bank of England promises to pay. These are trophies of detective skill, having been seized almost immediately they were exhibited by the ingenious makers. There also is the £5 note which was "out" for more than a hundred years, and which at compound interest had been to the Bank as good as £600. Likewise, the very neat-looking little note for £200 drawn for value received in "sugar-plums," presented, I believe, but not honoured. To these and others are added an objective history of Bank of England paper in specimens of notes of all values and dates.

The Board-room is spacious, sombre, and heavy with massive furniture and dense drapery. On the walls are pictures of William the Third, some of the earlier Georges, and a governor or two. The library is horrid with books on banking, money, exchanges, value theories, and currency. At this time of the year huge fires, each one big and fierce enough to roast an ox, are in every room and passage. In the large central room a furnace in a bay is faced by two great hooded chairs backed by a screen. At night—and all the night—two watchmen sit in those chairs and toast themselves. Their dreams, if they sleep, are likely enough to be uncanny, as hard by is the enclosure which was once a grave-yard, and there is a particular spot in the adjacent yard where, in the days of the "body-snatchers," some forty-five years ago, a Bank clerk was buried. This clerk was seven feet high, and well known to fame. He died, and it was believed that were he buried in any ordinary churchyard the resurrectionists would have him. There was no place as safe as the Bank. So his friends prayed the Board to grant him a resting-place within the Bank walls. The prayer was granted, and a most unusual deposit was paid in. It is highly probable that at night this ancient and much-honoured clerk stalks about room, corridor, and vault, and appears to the sleeping warders in the two hooded chairs.

Before leaving the Bank, visitors are favoured with a view of a splendid book of autographs. Each page is a note of fabulous value, and at the bottom of each leaf appears the name of some emperor, king, prince, noble ambassador, or very great personage. In time the book will be worth a fortune in itself. The Bank of England is a great show place; and seldom does a grandee come to the country without visiting it and without leaving in this volume his signature. The writing is sometimes curious, especially where a Japanese ambassador or a Persian Shah has scrawled his name in the characters of his native tongue, or where a Queen of Tahiti or a Khedive of Egypt has put a valued name to magnificent undertakings. Amongst the most interesting signatures are those of the young King of Spain and of the young son of the late Emperor of France. The last name entered is that of Thomas Burgers, President of the South African Republic of the Transvaal.

Having seen the whole Bank through, under the guidance of a gentleman as courteous as patient, we once more passed the detectives, and had stolen nothing.

GLADSTONE.

Only once have I had the good fortune to hear the foremost in the first rank of the public speakers of the day. Happily, my sole opportunity presented itself before the decision which withdrew from English political life the greatest of English statesmen. In was on a Saturday afternoon in the spring of the year, at the very eve of the elections which shattered the Liberal party and sent its chief into retirement, that I went to Woolwich to hear Mr. Gladstone address his supporters in that town. It was an open-air engagement—one of a series, a previous speech having been delivered at Blackheath. The day was fine and the crowd large. Probably there were fourteen thousand persons gathered together in Beresford Square. A wooden platform had been rigged up, large enough for a couple of hundred people. When I arrived, this elevation was crammed with the leading Woolwich Liberals and their wives and daughters; the roofs and windows of the neighbouring shops and houses were densely packed with overlookers, and the space in front of the hustings was already occupied by a tightly fitted mob. However, I screwed myself into a good position. The pressure upon the square inch was considerable, but I was able to endure it, sustained in part by the comfortable assurance that if somebody's elbows were deep in the small of my back, somebody's back felt the points of my elbows. Gladstone was due at three o'clock, but on this occasion he was not up to time. While waiting for him the crowd became facetious, but I cannot, Philistine though I be, re-crack their jokes on paper. The wit of a British mob consists chiefly in qualifying every person and thing by a hateful word, which seems to have been borrowed from the shambles, and is much more objectionable than the honest oaths which were picked up in Flanders. A really humorous remark was not dropped by a single person, in my hearing, at least. The badinage, notes, and comments were all as stupid as they were coarse. At last, after waiting half an hour in patient expectation, a roar came hoarsely down the main street, and I knew that the great man was coming. The mob stood on tip-toe, and cleared its throat for a lusty cheer. On Gladstone's appearance at the front of the hustings the lusty cheer broke forth, and some thousands of hats waved with an enthusiastic disregard of nap and brim. The People's William, the great minister, the brilliant financier, the copious orator, was before me. Photographs leave but little for the pen to do in the work of description. The Gladstone I saw in the flesh anybody may see who likes to spend a shilling on a good sun picture. A pale, lined face, a broad forehead, thatched with long, wispy, iron-grey hair, not over abundant, a nose well thrown out and capable of scorn, a mouth of great capacity and elastic lips, deep, bright, large flashing eyes, arched over by well-marked and flexible eyebrows, a visage stern, stormy, and forceful, an expression vehement and warlike, a head well poised, neck long, shoulders broad, arms lengthy, and stature tall, costume remarkable only in the blueness of the necktie—such was the Gladstone I saw. To my mind, unprejudiced by the ape theory, the great statesman looked very much like an eagle of royal breed. And when the orator kindled with his talk, as the eye shot forth its vivid glances and the clenched hands struck out with a rapid forward thrust, the aquiline likeness was the closer. In a particular passage of his speech, in which he attacked an adventurous Mr. Liardet and a poor Mr. Boord, Landseer's picture of the eagles in the swannery was brought to my mind, more especially the battle in mid-air, where one fierce warrior bird is delivering with concentrated force a mortal blow to its soft and sinking prey. The first thing Mr. Gladstone did was to take a modest and evidently medicinal drink from an elegant little bottle, upon which some voices in the crowd shouted "Gin!" while other voices, in wrath at the ignoble insinuation, shouted "Shame!" These little preliminaries over, Mr. Gladstone began with a husky voice, as if the Blackheath speech had made his throat sore. This at once explained the appeal to the elegant little bottle, and placed the "gin" libel beyond even Conservative belief. Husky although it was, the voice rang out with a full, intelligible sound into the ears of the vast crowd. The chairman had made an introductory speech, not one word of which had I heard—no, not a syllable. The spectacle of a somewhat small but highly respectable gentleman gesticulating and beating the air with much vehemence over a noiseless nothing was at once amusing and disheartening. I could not help laughing at the little man's dumb show, but the miserable thought possessed me that, as I could not hear the chairman, so I could not hear Gladstone. But the first word dispelled the fear. The large, powerful, and, excepting the huskiness, sound organs of the orator's speech gave out the word "Gentlemen!" as with the force of a triple bob-major. The mob was electrified. He spoke nearly sixty minutes, and not a sentence was lost. Towards the close, when the subject-matter of the address admitted of some warmth of treatment, the voice cleared itself of its hoarseness at a bound and sprang out clear and sharp into the air, quivering as it went with an emotional vibration and a passionate fervour. The speech itself was not, I should say, one of Gladstone's best. It was by no means equal in any one respect to the Greenwich oration. The, at that time, famous Malacca Straits had been sailed through and exhausted, and all that he could venture upon was to splash a little of the Straits' water into Mr. Disraeli's face. Having met that morning with a timely squib, he gave it, and gave it well, as follows:—

> "The farmers at Aylesbury gathered to dine,
> And they ate their prime beef and they drank their old wine;
> With the wine there was beer, with the beer there was bacca.
> The liquors went round, and the banquet was crowned
> With some thundering news from the Straits of Malacca."

This morsel Gladstone recited, rather than read, with a mighty roll and much appreciation of the fun, elongating the "Straits of Malacca" as a gourmand prolongs the pleasure of a tit-bit, and smacked his lips after it with unhesitating delight. The crowd enjoyed it also. Indeed, the "Straits of Malacca" was the richest joke out in that day. This was pretty well the only laughing matter in the speech. There was, however, another. A story from the middle ages was introduced to throw the light of ridicule upon the Conservative policy of nullity and the Conservative organization. There were, once upon a time, some casuists who boasted of their ability to cause legions of angels to dance upon the point of a needle. So the Conservative leaders seemed to be ambitious to make legions of voters dance upon a needle's point, and if not on a needle's point, then in thin air. The story was told with effect, and was danced over by the mob with great glee. These were the levities of the address. The opening remarks were mere statements explanatory of the reasons why he had not resigned his seat on accepting the Chancellorship of the Exchequer, and of Dockyard management, and the peroration was an appeal to all sections of the Liberal party in behalf of union, on the ground of practical wisdom. But it is the man and the manner I am endeavouring in this slight sketch to recall, not the substance of the speech. The statements were clear and lucid, in no wise clouded by words or entangled in parentheses; and the appeal was, if not powerful, dignified. The orator's work was made disagreeable to him, and the effect of his speech was marred somewhat by the enemy. The Conservatives were strong in Woolwich, and they certainly showed a very striking display of force on Saturday afternoon. They brayed and hissed with a vigour which did them credit and harassed Mr. Gladstone very much. Again and again was he reduced to momentary silence, and as often as that was the case did he shrug his shoulders in disgust and dart indignant glances at the yelling foe. "Go on!" shouted his friends; "never mind them!" But he did mind them, and he was especially aggravated by an impudent young Tory who insisted upon making a counter-speech from the standpoint of a licensed victualler's balcony. For some time the speech of the Premier appeared to be echoed back with a beery difference from the tavern walls. At last, however, the youngster was silenced by a shower of Liberal oranges and eggs, after which Mr. Gladstone had his own sweet will, and gave the crowd a taste of his powers. The speech began a little after three in the afternoon and came to a close a little after four. I do not consider that I heard the orator at his best. The foemen were not worthy of his steel. Swans and geese scarcely excite the great fighting powers of an eagle. Still, I thank my good stars that while Gladstone was yet a passionate politician I had the chance of listening to his voice.

SPURGEON.

One day I went very early to the Tabernacle, breaking the Sabbath in a very disagreeable manner in the inside of an omnibus, in order not to be too late. Spurgeon ought to take his stand in a more central place than the neighbourhood of the Elephant and Castle. The pulpit of St. Paul's would be more accommodating, and certainly, on personal experience, I can say that he would fill and grace it far better than a Canon whom I once heard there. A worse sermon—one more deficient in elevated sentiment and manly thought—I have seldom heard than that reverend gentleman wagged his head over on the day which unfortunately I selected for a visit to London's great cathedral. It was by no means a deliverance after the manner of the sacramental or ritualistic school. In some respects it was, perhaps, strictly evangelical. But it treated the great personage of Christianity and His sufferings in a method that may be called surgical, and associated the Deity with parts of His human frame and with the penalties they bore, in the manner of an empiric attempting a diagnosis, or of an Augur peering into the viscera of a victim in search of a sacred meaning. The pulpit of St. Paul's should always have a man in it. I believe it generally has, but I was unfortunate enough to be there when a mere phraser was in possession.

On reaching the Tabernacle, I found myself, with a hundred others, on the wrong side of an iron rail. A janitor, very likely a deacon, was at the gate, whose duty it was to tell strangers that at a certain minute they could enter if they had a passport. I speedily possessed myself of this requisite, on application to another deacon with a bag, and discovered it to be a neat little envelope, with an inscription to the effect that a donation, put in the envelope and deposited in a box hard by, would be thankfully received by the treasurer of the Tabernacle College for Theological Students. At the appointed time, in I went, penetrating to the very centre of the huge room. Strangers, I was informed, were not to invade the pews, but to seat themselves in the aisles on little movable shelves or brackets, attached by hinge and strut to the pew ends. These contrivances are clever, but uncomfortable. However, I beguiled the time before the regular congregation came, in friendly gossip with an old lady who had evidently been sent on to take care of a pew and keep out intruders. She informed me sympathetically that "he had been bootiful that morning." I learnt from her also that the Tabernacle seated eight thousand and could hold ten. This was possibly an estimate made in the spirit of a new company's prospectus; but the room looked large enough to justify the old lady's enthusiastic arithmetic. The vast floor, pewed from wall to wall, the spacious double galleries curving round the oval, the two platforms, one for the baptistery and the other for the preacher's desk, both crowded with chairs, produced the impression of a most liberal accommodation. The place, which seemed monstrous in its length, height, and breadth of cubic space, was clear of pillar or arch, choir or organ, being wholly given up to the simple idea of inviting and holding a crowd. And the sense of size was aggravated by the fact that this immense room was no hall of council in which hundreds of men would share in debate, no theatre on whose stage a little multitude of actors would strut and mouth, no concert-room with a choir of a thousand voices, but a chapel in which just one man would hold sway with his single tongue. The next thought was that of course the single tongue in this case must be necessarily one of most unusual qualities.

The Tabernacle is undoubtedly a wonderful witness for Spurgeon. It must be taken for granted that the man for whom the Tabernacle was built is a man of his own kind. Cathedrals are certainly more massive, but they were erected for the grandeur of a national religion, for the love of greatness in art, and for a splendid worship of ceremonies and choral power. The Tabernacle was built for a preacher to preach in; and as long as it stands it will be a memorial of the fact that there was in the middle of the 19th century a preacher with a voice like a clarion and with a spirit of sympathy and wisdom to teach him what to do with his voice so that men should come to hear and listen. The large building was evidence of this to me, while it was empty of all but the strangers in the aisles, and while as yet the preacher was still taking his preparatory cup of tea, or whatever it might be, in the vestry. I could not help speculating, however, on what may become of the Tabernacle when its present master leaves it. It will be of no use for a parson with a big voice to bellow platitudes, or prettinesses, or mysticisms, from the tribune. Emptiness and echoes will, in that case, take the place of the present crowd. The monstrous place will always demand a special man, and the demand will very likely not always be met. In almost every particular that may be mentioned but one there are many preachers in England head and shoulders above Spurgeon—many of more accurate mind, many of truer wisdom, many of greater culture, many of a finer spirit, many of wider knowledge, many of a more penetrating insight, many of a more stirring eloquence, many of a broader sympathy, and some, perhaps, of a higher purpose, but they fall short of Spurgeon in that one thing, whatever it may be, which makes a man the sovereign of a multitude; and that one thing, let it be simple or complex, is a rare gift. When a man has it, people build a Tabernacle for him, and he fills it. When he dies the Tabernacle through all its windows looks out inquiringly for a successor, and is pretty sure to look in vain. It is impossible to say that the Tabernacle, like the *Great Eastern*, is a mistake, because the big chapel answers its intended purpose. But when the giant departs into the shadow of the past, the chances are that the wind only will whistle through the bars of his helmet. Smaller men will shrink from the ridicule and odious comparison which would make them dwarfs. It is true that the *Great Eastern*, having been unsuccessful as an ocean passenger and merchant ship for the million, has found occupation as a cable tank. This suggests the possibility of the Tabernacle finding a new purpose when the present one is no longer answered for want of a successor to the Boanerges for whom it was built. It would be a pity to see a chimney rear its ugly length upon that roof; and it would be as great a pity to hear a locomotive screeching under that ceiling; a greater still to see a stage hero stalk across that platform, or a clown grin from that floor, or a ballet girl dance on that baptistery! Probably, however, desecration will be avoided by the free use of partitions. The Tabernacle could easily be apportioned into twelve ordinary churches, and it would be a beneficial spectacle to society were the denominations to have at least one temple devoted to union to the extent, at all events, of a common roof, for a dozen pulpits.

By the hour of the service the chapel was crowded. Not only were the seats occupied, but the aisles were full. Look which way I would there were no vacant places. How many persons were actually present I cannot say. If my friend, the old lady, was right, there must have been eight thousand. But I can hardly accept her computation as correct. It was, however, evident that Spurgeon has to-day all his early powers of commanding congregations. He draws still. And this may be taken as proof that his power is real honest strength, and not the fitful force of spasm. His popularity has its foundations firmly laid in the depths of nature, and not in the glittering surface shallows of mere art or artifice. It was a bold venture to build a chapel so immense, and would have been a sorry blunder had he for whom it was built been a man of limited means or, to borrow language from the turf, of feeble staying powers. The room there is in the Tabernacle for empty pews is alarming to any one with an imagination. A thousand souls might be lost, beyond hue and cry, in that pit and those galleries. A small but select congregation would be a ridiculous failure within those walls. Sheer substance and strength can alone have avoided a disaster in this respect. The disaster has been avoided; the Tabernacle continues to attract; and the fact is better proof of Spurgeon's genuineness than any criticism of his style of work can supply.

The congregation seated, and the clock hand upon the hour, in came the preacher and announced the hymn. The arrangement for lighting the room by gas threw him into the shade, or failed at all events to light up his face. I could but see that Spurgeon was an Englishman in bulk and figure, the visage being full and bluff. Like all men of much force, he is not particularly handsome. His costume was not clerical, and his cravat was not white. As he stood behind the open rail of the platform, with no lights about him, he seemed dark, burly, ill-defined. Out of this vagueness, however, came a voice of singular clearness and command—not a deep, guttural voice from painful depths, not a shrill, high-sounding shallow voice, but an utterance of sustained melody, far-reaching, and everywhere itself. I suppose every one in the chapel, not deaf, heard every word the preacher said from the moment he opened his mouth.

At an early part of the service Spurgeon had to give notice that on a day mentioned the Reverend Newman Hall would lecture in the Tabernacle, on behalf of his new church. What Spurgeon said was, " The Reverend Newman Hall will lecture on behalf of his new chapel, or church, or what he calls it." The word " church " came out with a grunt, and the phrase " or what he calls it " was a contemptuous protest against " churching " anything but the elect. The manner in which this formal notice was read disclosed the spirit of the man—not a bitter spirit, but one of much self-assertion. He could not read out poor Newman Hall's innocent little bill without biting at what he conceived to be an un-Tabernacleish and anti-Spurgeonic use of an ecclesiastical term. I cannot say I sympathized with the prayer. This was my fault, no doubt. But it was apparently couched in the language of expostulation and command. Something of this may be due to the fact that the speaker is accustomed to lead the devotions of seven or eight thousand from an elevated platform; and, again, something is possibly to be attributed to the influence of doctrinal views of assurance and election. When the Almighty was invoked, by " His signet and His bracelet," to come and fulfil His promise, the reference seemed unsuitable and unedifying, to say the least. The Lesson was the chapter on the call of Samuel, and was not read without explanatory remarks. On coming to the passage in which Eli's dimness of sight is referred to, Spurgeon said, "An old annotator has observed that this was a punishment on the old man for winking at the evil conduct of his sons." The name of the old annotator was not mentioned; but the conceit was received by the congregation as authentic and authoritative.

The sermon was on Samuel's response to the Divine call—"Here am I." It is no part of my intention to follow the discourse through all its parts. The truth is, I have forgotten the "divisions" and cannot recall the "skeleton." The Spurgeonisms of the sermon alone remain with me, together with the general impressions that I was in the presence of a workman who knew, in all he said, whether what he said was humorous or pathetic, grotesque or plainly wise, didactic or enthusiastic, how to deal with human nature, especially with the men and women who, by natural selection or by gracious election, crowd, Sunday by Sunday, to the Tabernacle. Very possibly the particular bits of the sermon which I am alone able to reproduce may not communicate my impressions to others, as they will chiefly represent that part of Spurgeon which some will consider to be his deformity and his weakness. To this I can only say that humour and bold outspokenness suit the English people. The Tabernacle was not built for the cultivated or for men of taste, and Spurgeon is not the Apostle of "sweetness and light," but has an especial mission to the Philistine. And what, I may ask, are the four millions in London made of, and what is to touch them? Taste is a very pretty thing, and much to be desired, but it is unavoidably limited in its distribution by the great facts of human life, so many of us having to get our living by selling sugar, brewing beer, making shoes, digging coals, costermongering, and writing for newspapers. No man will become a great preacher who has a devotion to taste. Preachers have to work with the roughest material of human nature and society, and are not artists those whose duty it is to discover and represent beauty. Of course there is a division of labour in pulpit work. London has several preachers whose sermons are the very flower of cultivated intellect, acceptable to the most refined. They have their place, but the masses would learn no more from them than they would from the south-west wind blowing ever so softly and sweetly through blossoming trees.

Spurgeon had something to say about the wisdom of placing children early under religious influences, and combated those who would hold them back. "What," said he, "do you London flower-growers do when these gentle spring showers fall? Do you put out the larger plants only to catch the blessing, or the small with the large? You place them all under the life-giving rain. Do the same with children. When Heaven drops its fatness or distils its dew put out your little pots—yes, put out your little pots." Speaking of excuses for neglect of Church work, he said that some who were very busy he should be very glad to excuse, and spoke very pointedly to those excellent ladies who were "diligent in their attendance at Dorcas meetings, but forgot to sew the buttons on to their husbands' shirts." Upon this there was a slight rustling of millinery throughout the Tabernacle, and I observed that several ladies looked at several other ladies to see how the needle pricked. The hardest part of obedience was, he remarked, a hearty response to a call to suffer. Some could yield cheerfully, and he quoted, by way of example, Dr. Hamilton's—I think it was Dr. Hamilton's—"Betty." "The heavenly voice said, 'Betty, take care of those five little children,' and Betty replied, 'Here am I.' Then the voice said, 'Betty, take care of your sick old husband,' and Betty replied, 'Here am I.' At last the voice said, 'Betty, lie down on that bed for years, and cough,' and Betty said, 'Here am I,' and she lay down and coughed to the glory of God." Then Spurgeon added a little from his own experience. He had been bound to his bed. He had tried hard to say, "Here am I," and had forced the words out, but he had found himself saying, "Yes, here I am; but, Lord, let me get up as soon as possible! I much prefer working to suffering."

His concluding five minutes were devoted to an elaborate consolation of those who supposed that in heaven the Divine solicitude would be given only to the men of renown in the Church—the public preacher or the famous saint. Such would assuredly not be the case. "Look," said he, "to a home at Christmas time. The fire blazes merrily on the hearth; the table is richly spread; around is every sign of festive happiness; but there is one thing missing—it is the rosy face of the little toddling one of the house. On this discovery will the mother say, 'Oh, it is all right; she has perhaps gone to bed!' Or will the father say, 'Never mind; we shall find her to-morrow!' Or should a visitor come in and say, 'Why all this fuss about the young one? have you not the sparkling log and the joyous feast? and are you not here yourselves?' Would they cease their searching? You know they would not, but would ransack every hole and corner to find the little darling. So, were the meanest child of the Father missing in heaven, He would stop the harps of all the angels to shout the name of the lost one, and would sweep heaven empty to find him." These things lose all their pathos in the telling, just as a cut flower withers in the hand. In the Tabernacle, on my Sunday there, a hundred people, poor in spirit, seemed very much cheered by this Christmas parable. The intentness of the great concourse all through the sermon hour was remarkable. No eyes seemed to wander away from the preacher except those of the professional note-taker, who had to watch effect on others rather than on himself. Upon the whole, one learns from a service at the Tabernacle that greatness and narrowness can keep company, and that work is good work just as it suits. I am not anxious to hear Spurgeon many more times, but I shall be glad to know that his chapel, or church, or tabernacle, or "what he calls it," is always crowded. It would also be satisfactory to find ten Tabernacles in London were there ten Spurgeons to fill them. But a preacher to crowds is a rare bird.

DR. PARKER.

Written in 1875.

There is probably no place of public worship in London so largely attended by men as the City Temple. This opinion is founded upon several observations made chiefly on Sundays. Dr. Parker gives morning lectures on Thursdays, professedly to City men, and on these occasions the cynical only would expect many bonnets. I am not referring to these week-day exercises, but to the regular Sunday services. It is well known to be all but universally the case that our churches and chapels are frequented more by women than men. The City Temple is one of the exceptions. Pew after pew is often filled entirely with representatives of the irreligious sex. Last Sunday I counted ten men in one of the gallery seats, half a dozen in another, and similar instances of the same kind in the floor pews. This, of course, lessens the artistic effect of a City Temple congregation. Men, when massed together, especially in their best clothes, are sadly wanting in picturesqueness. Colour is wholly absent. The Sabbath male costume is simply hideous. The ten men in the one seat to which I referred just now was one of the most depressing sights I had seen for some time. How Dr. Parker, who has to face a score of such ugly groups, manages to smile so radiantly and so often as he does is a mystery. If men will go to church in such numbers they certainly should shave so as to display their cravats, which, together with their vests, should be of some brilliant colour and gay device. Modern modes of showing respect in worship do not admit of a covering for male heads, or the fez or turban would be a great improvement in most cases, more especially as almost every middle-aged Englishman has lost his hair.

But this prevalence of men in the City Temple has a relation to other things than the lust of the eye. It suggests that the service has especial attractions for that class. This must be granted to be really the case. It is no accident which gathers so many beards together from time to time in a particular building. It must be acknowledged that there is some power in the City Temple which draws men thither in larger proportions than elsewhere, and undoubtedly the power, whatever it is, has its centre in the pulpit. The City Temple service is all pulpit. There is no ritual. Besides, as a rule, men do not care much about ritual. The singing is congregational and very full-bodied. There is to be a very splendid organ by-and-by, but at present an energetic gentleman, who beats vigorous time with his hymn-book from the gallery behind the pulpit, leads the psalmody, which, if fairly good, can scarcely be said to be the particular attraction to the men who crowd to the church on the Viaduct. The Temple itself is a fine room inside—spacious and well proportioned—but it is only a fine room, and there are many rooms much finer. The explanation must be sought for in the pulpit—not, of course, in the handsome and stately piece of furniture which, I believe, the City Corporation presented to the Temple on its opening; although it is, in its beauty of form and colour, and the ampleness of its size, worthy of admiration. On the opening day, now nearly two years ago, this platform of marble was indeed peculiarly attractive, from the singular adornments which were most artistically worked into the open spaces between the supporting pillars, and placed upon the cornices of the desk. The wealth of some conservatory had been transferred to the City Temple pulpit, which glowed with the fresh beauty of living flowers. Had this ornamentation been continued, it would be possible to pretend that the gentlemen who frequent the Temple in such unusual numbers do so from a love of floral decoration. As, however, the plants were all removed when the opening services were concluded, this is a solution of the problem which cannot be advanced. There is but one admissible solution, and it can only be found in the occupant of the pulpit. Dr. Parker is unquestionably a fisher of men. At all events, he catches them. Why? Is it because he himself is eminently masculine? Certainly this does not necessarily follow, any more than that he "who rules our freemen must himself be free," or, "who buys fat oxen must himself be fat." Feminine qualities are, in many cases, remarkably dominant over men. They will go in hosts to hear a Jenny Lind sing, and in crowds to see a Taglioni dance. But let it be said at once that there is no evidence to show that they will throng to listen to speechifying, lecturing, or preaching women. There is no basis of fact and precedent for the supposition that an eloquent female, because she is a female as well as eloquent, would be permanently and especially attractive to men. One or two restaurants in the City appear to thrive on female waiters; but waiting is a woman's function. Preaching is not. Ladies are quite equal to the work of qualifying themselves for a Doctor's degree in Divinity, but I question whether they have the stuff of which a preacher, popular with men, is made; although, as I have already admitted, it does not necessarily follow that because men are attracted by a particular style of pulpit work that it must, on that account, be manly in the best sense of that word.

Still, let what may be said about the reason, the fact remains that Dr. Parker is a man's preacher. There are some pulpit orators in London who are women's preachers, and again, some who are preachers to children. They are respectively attractive to the classes indicated, and it is reasonable to suppose that they are in mental and moral harmony and sympathy with those whose attention they command. Is it unreasonable to suppose that Dr. Parker's specialty has a similar foundation? It can scarcely be denied that men go to hear the great-voiced Doctor because he suits men—suits a great many men—and suits them because there is a certain substance of manhood in him and an air of manliness about him. I have approached this conclusion by steps, and not at a bound, because some critics have said, " Yes, the voice is the voice of Joseph—Dr. Joseph; but the hands are the hands of Esau;" meaning by this that the effects at the City Temple are not the products of genuineness and simplicity. Now, where these are absent, where is true manhood? But will men in unusual numbers persevere in attending a preacher who is merely dexterous, or imposing, or superficially brilliant? It may be said that this is possible with some classes of men. For my part I must adhere to the opinion of those who think that flashiness has no lasting dominion over men of any class. As a rule men speedily slip off from polished surfaces or break through painted air-bubbles. The only proper treatment due to a succession of facts, or to a fact of tenacious continuity, is, in the first place, acceptance; and, in the second, the allowance of a logical position. The fact of Dr. Parker's long popularity with men does not fit in with the notion that he is a pulpit trickster.

The preacher at the City Temple does not ignore the modern spirit of inquiry which, beginning in doubt, enlarges the dominion of scepticism with every new discovery. Our Doctor is not afraid to let it be known that he is aware of the doings of science, literature, and criticism, and of the destructive conquests they claim to be making over venerable theory and venerated dogma. He will not allow his pulpit or his church to be a fool's paradise. Let others close their eyes to the facts of the day and preach as though the characteristics of the last age were the conditions of the present time, he will not. It is his opinion that a preacher should recognize the advance of theological and metaphysical thought as carefully as a statesman notes the march of events and the development of political ideas, or as a City man follows the changes of the money market and studies the novelties of commercial enterprise. Dr. Parker does not consider it to be the wisest course to be silent in the Temple about those very subjects relating to religious belief which men talk most about upon the Viaduct. He knows that great changes are occurring in the temper with which men treat theological inquiry as well as in the opinions they are gradually shaping into new creeds, and he is courageous enough not to play the part of the ostrich in the presence of his congregation. If a fascinating book, out of the old style—"Ecce Homo," to wit—is sold by booksellers and sells well, he will admit the fact, and would not greatly object to produce a copy and wave it before the eyes of his people. Let a profound thinker—call him Herbert Spencer or any other name—give a new direction to the movement of speculative intellect, our Doctor will not affect to treat him with silent contempt, but will rather announce his appearance, as promptly as Madame Tussaud heralds the installation of a new effigy in her chamber of horrors. He will not let the City Temple think that he is afraid to meet the enemies of Zion in the gate. Probably this is one reason why men in more than the ordinary numbers attend his ministry. It is unquestionably the case that all those men who are fully alive to the movement of the time along the line of speculation feel a contempt for the pulpits which show no sign of any recognition of important facts. It is not at all wonderful that such men will prefer to listen to a man who fashions his Sunday talk in accordance with their Monday questionings and experiences. The most valued watch-dog is he who barks at the passing step, and not he who bays at the distant moon.

But if it is excellent in a preacher to point to dangers and detect the enemy, it is more excellent to be able to settle questions, and show the way to victory. Dr. Parker is a preacher of this kind. He meets "Ecce Homo" with "Ecce Deus." He himself confronts Herbert Spencer. It was my good fortune to make one of a large congregation one Sunday morning when he put the author of "First Principles" utterly to shame. The Doctor announced that he had heard much about a certain chapter in a great work which purported to discuss the greatest question of theology. He had, he said, obtained that book, read it, read the chapter through and through. And what, he asked, was it but "words—words—words?" What was the laboured outcome of the whole argument but that God was "The Unknowable?" "Why?" said the triumphant Doctor, with a twinkle in his eye, and a smile of superb superiority in every dimple, "I could have told the philosopher that at the cost of 'a shilling telegram.'" The conquest was complete. Herbert Spencer collapsed. I was able to feel that the whole congregation had that wordy gentleman under their feet. He was rolled over and over in the dust of the City Temple, and was expelled at the door with much laughter. Another day the Doctor had the Deluge for his subject, and he was equally severe with those bold men who deny the flood and with those who went peering about into caves and climbing to the tops of mountains to support the Bible narrative with a shell. To him, the Deluge was one of the universal events of human history and life. It was now in fact, if not in form, round and about the world—the fulfilment of the law by which destruction follows transgression. He did not want their shells. Nor was he troubled to settle with himself whether the rain was all over the world in the days of Noah. It was enough for him, as it was with Noah, to observe what took place from his own window. As to those who would not hear the Deluge story at all, what had they to say about the judgments and punishments of the passing day! "O fools, and slow of heart to believe!" Then there were those fastidious critics who were so very particular about the Ark, and who had showed with their carpenter's rule and the rule of three that it was an impossibility—what was to be said about them? Clearly no narrative would have pleased them. Had Noah and his family been divinely empowered to walk upon the waters, they would have talked about the "natural buoyancy" of the human frame; and here the Doctor admirably imitated the process of floating, puffed his gown out into the dimensions of a Boyton swimming dress, and achieved a complete victory over the base realist. This is the way in which the modern Doubting Castle is overthrown by the Greatheart of the City Temple. And, probably, this is another reason why some men put themselves under his care with so much readiness. There are several classes of speculative men, and a large class is composed of individuals who long for a strong bold man to laugh at the laughers, criticize the critics, and put the cap and bells upon the philosophers, and of other individuals who desire to be comforted with the assurance that their old things are as reasonable, as scientific, and based as much on first principles, as the new. The members of this class may not be in the first rank of intelligent thinkers; but they are very numerous, and they are not difficult to satisfy. And our Doctor is the very man to give them the satisfaction they crave. With an epigram—in Herbert Spencer's case, with a telegram—he can slaughter a theory; with a sarcasm he can poniard a philosopher; and with a laugh he can turn rationalism into ridicule. It is a pleasure to watch the faces of the congregation as the rich, resounding, confident voice plays its clever feats with the catch-words of modern wisdom. Every man seems animated with a sublime disdain of the critics. Doubts are after all but bubbles, which the breath of their Doctor can blow about at his pleasure and burst at his will.

Dr. Parker's courage is by no means limited to the region of theological speculation. As the manager of a Church, and as a public man having a public position, he is enterprising and demonstrative. A master of style has wedded the epithet "bad" with the epithet "bold" in a description of Cromwell, more remarkable for vigour of expression than for strictness in truth. Such is the vital force of smart speech that it continues to live and reign long after it has been proved to be false. In this case, not only is it too commonly believed that Cromwell really was "bold and bad," but it has become impossible to say of any man that he is bold, without at once suggesting that he is also bad. Were it not for this taking trick of alliteration, I should, without hesitation, say that Dr. Parker is a bold man—bold in every public capacity which he fills. Boldness is something more than courage, bravery, or spirit. It is all that is meant by those words, with the qualities of aggressiveness and self-assertion superadded. A merely brave man may never meet with the circumstances fitted to call forth and manifest his latent powers. A bold man makes his own circumstances, if necessary; and, like the strolling tragedy-hero, carries his stage with him. Mr. Disraeli is a capital example of the bold man. He has not only the courage essential to his career, but he has the ability and the will to secure a platform for his great performances. At the moment of a terrible failure he prophesied his brilliant success. When honourable members were laughing him into silence, he, like the ancient seers of his race, lifted up his voice, and said "that the time should come when they should hear him." Since that day he has been diligently fulfilling his own prediction by making opportunity. His matchless feat has been the education of the Conservative party into a cleverly managed troupe, skilfully prepared to play up to the great part he has chosen for himself. Had he been a brave man only, he would now be writing novels and leading articles. Boldness has been his promotion. Mr. Gladstone is not bold, or he would not now be in retreat. He is heroically courageous, and can work wonders, if the nation and the Parliament will give him space for his vast strides and sweeping blows; but if there is no free course kept for him, he will retire and turn sword and club into a woodman's axe. Dr. Parker and Mr. Disraeli are very different personages in many respects, no doubt; but they are both bold; and this is probably one reason why they are both favourites with men.

Only a bold man would plant his pulpit upon the Viaduct. Just at the very time when ancient City churches are being pulled down because their congregations have long since gone to the suburbs, Dr. Parker selects for the site of his Temple a place upon the highway of traffic, in the midst of markets, railway stations, prisons, offices, warehouses, and shops. The ordinary idea is that churches must follow homes, and go where people live. Our Doctor's plan is to pay no attention to these things, and fix himself in a good advertising position, confident that, if he can only let it be known where he preaches, people will come to him. The confidence must have been of the first order of magnitude which determined upon the venture of spending, I know not how many scores of thousands, upon a preaching place on the Holborn Viaduct—a place in which the sermon should be the only attraction, unaccompanied by splendour of ritual or charm of music. I scarcely know of any modern act of larger audacity, unless it be the purchase of the Suez Canal shares by Mr. Disraeli. The

Baptist, it is true, sought the wilderness, when he cried aloud to the generation of his day. But the City on a Sunday is a more unfavourable place for a congregation than the wilderness of Judæa. While the Temple was yet being built, it might have been thought by an intelligent stranger that a provision was being made by some eccentric millionaire for a Sabbath refuge for the unfortunate statues on the Viaduct, doomed all the working day of the week to the wear and tear of a ceaseless traffic. They could not escape to suburban residences, semi-detached and detached villas on the Sunday, and the Temple was rising close to them in friendly neighbourhood. To an intelligent stranger, I say, the two facts might have been suggestive. But the Doctor knew what he was about—that is to say, he knew himself. Give him a good stand on the Viaduct, and he was sure that the people would gather together unto him. In point of fact he gave himself the good stand, and thus he is, by this sign, one of the boldest men of the day.

The same quality was exhibited in the ceremonies with which the Temple was opened. Dr. Parker may, I presume, be counted as belonging to the descendants of the Puritans. Yet he welcomed to his celebrations the Lord Mayor, in all his glory of robe, chain, and mace; while his spacious pulpit, built of marble from the land of the Pope, was a gift from the Corporation of London, and was smothered in flowers plentiful enough for a year's floral decorations for St. Alban's, and in the evening there was a Dean to his tea-meeting. All this is the work of a man who is brave enough to choose his own surroundings and to build up his own standing-place. Puritanism is history and precedent; but Dr. Parker is to be a man of the day and his own authority. He, therefore, on opening the Temple, calls to his side as much of the State as there may be in a Lord Mayor's coach, as much of Church as there may be in a Dean of Westminster, and as much of the World as there may be in hot-house flowers. This is boldness. But the boldest part of it is that Dr. Parker thus signifies that Puritanism is of the past, and that in his Temple services and fashions are to be seen in the form and manner in which the religious spirit is to accommodate itself to the social life of the day. Church, State, and the World are not to the spiritual man what they were a century or two ago, so the spiritual man can welcome a little pomp, shake hands with an Erastian, and preach out of a pulpit quarried near Rome and blooming like a bouquet. Dr. Parker is bold enough to be a Reformer. He is one. He is now originating the Puritan Catholic Church, that is to say, a Church combining a consciousness of personal liberty and responsibility in its members with a willingness to recognize the brotherhood of other Churches in which authority is considered to be as important as individual freedom.

The bold reforming tendency of Dr. Parker is to be seen very clearly in his endeavour to bring about an exchange of pulpits between Conformist and Nonconformist preachers. If this is not the result of a desire to have old things fitted to new conditions and the new spirit in English common life, then it is only a piece of personal vanity aiming at promotion, and a foolish vanity aiming at impossible promotion. This explanation I, for one, cannot accept, because it does not explain other peculiarities in the Doctor's ways which are to be explained by the theory that the City Temple is also a Reformer.

Just as the part played by the Lord Mayor, and the welcome given to the Dean at the opening services, indicate a softening of the Puritan heart towards Church and State, so the presence of a whole conservatory of flowers beneath, around, and upon the pulpit, may be accepted as an explanation of that other modification of Puritanism in the direction of elasticism—to coin a word—which enabled the City Temple to widen itself out to embrace Mr. Ward Beecher. Flowers on a Puritan pulpit indicate, perhaps, a greater change in spirit than tolerance of a civic or an ecclesiastical dignitary. In this case they may be taken as showing a large admixture of human nature with the gifts of grace. Old Puritanism would have thrown the flowers to the dunghill, and consigned the Plymouth-pulpiter to perdition. The City Temple Puritanism finds that nosegays give a beauty to worship, and that Charity is not to be scouted when she suffereth long and is kind. Probably, however, Dr. Parker was in his boldest temper when he sent his sympathetic telegram to the Plymouth Church.

It is, I think, not unfair to say that the boldness of Dr. Parker becomes audacity in the City Temple pulpit. His presence, manner, and style would be startling on any platform, or in any public walk in life. Were he to enter the House of Commons, his luxuriant growth of hair, his all-pervading smile, his unrestrained gestures and nervous action, his mighty, tempestuous voice, his thundering epigrams, and flashing sarcasm, his laugh, let loose to the winds, and his mental and oratorical *abandon*, would be considered to be sensational. Now, the pulpit has been thought to demand a heavier and duller decorum than the floor of the House. Dr. Parker, however, does not think so, or he takes to himself the liberty of being an exception. His nature is rich in force and in variety, and he sees no reason why he should narrow and restrain himself in his office as a preacher. Nature having given him a wealth of locks capable of graceful arrangement, why should he submit to the tonsure or to the Puritanic roundheadedness? Luxuriance of hair becomes the orator. Possessing a voice —and that a mighty voice—why should he soften and sweeten it into meek lispings and curate-like cooings? Having a smile which flows forth from each corner of the mouth in eddies and dimples, widening and circling until the whole Temple is full of them and every face reflects them, why should he cultivate the grace of sourness for especial Sabbath use? Having a great laugh, why should he not, when reproving scorners, let it go forth as a terror and a storm into their ears? Or why, when he triumphs, should he not rise to the highest notes in the gamut of joyfulness? It being natural to him to feel his thoughts at his very fingers' ends, why should he, when he warms to his subject, keep his hands pinned to his side while every nerve tingles, and every muscle is eager for action? Similarly, if the humorous side of his topic presents itself, he sees no reason why he should be ashamed to look at it or to turn it round so that the congregation might see it also. Humour is natural to men, and, if not a grace, is a gift, and a gift which need not be hidden by pulpit walls, smothered under preacher's gown, or choked by his bands. Having the ability to make "points," Dr. Parker makes them. He has no notion that pulpit oratory should be unassisted by the art of putting things. That it should be said that he is "dramatic," or "theatrical," or even "stagey," is not terrible to him; because he takes such criticisms to mean that he endeavours to be as effective as possible and lays tribute on all his powers. Dr. Parker, in fact, takes the liberty to go into the City Temple pulpit as the natural man, and not as a professional person—trimmed, subdued, barbered, swathed, and drilled into a portentous propriety. He has not, it is true, discarded the gown and bands, and that he has not done so is to be taken as a sign that he has not entirely emancipated himself from the fashions of the clerical caste.

The free use which Dr. Parker allows himself to make of all his varied powers is justified by his success. The outward and visible sign of a preacher's efficiency is his congregation. A large audience is in this case a measure of force. It is but a trick to say that Mr. Henry Irving or Mr. John Toole would draw a larger number of persons to the City Temple were Dr. Parker, in his liberality in the interchange of platforms, to permit either of those gentlemen to officiate for him. The attracting force in the case of a professional actor occupying a pulpit would be merely curiosity, or a sense of the grotesque in an incongruous association. Were either the tragedian or the comedian to change his work and turn preacher, and continuously command the crowds which frequent the City Temple, the case would simply be the case of Dr. Parker—that of attraction by force. For my part I do not think that Mr. Irving could ever excel as a preacher were he to become one by conviction of duty. Mr. Toole might, as, notwithstanding Sir Robert Carden's dictum while hearing the late case of libel, "that no one ever shed a tear when he saw Mr. Toole play," he is no doubt as capable of pathos as he is of drollery, and would be sure to show his capacity in this respect were he impelled to serious work by a sense of duty or by a new enthusiasm. Whether as a preacher, Mr. Toole, had he been one from the beginning, would have rivalled the success of Dr. Parker, would depend probably upon whether he would have adopted the plan of Dr. Parker and set his whole self to the task. Dr. Parker has done this, and one of the crowning rewards of his labour is that from Sunday to Sunday more than 2,000 people flock to him, although his stand is, as I have already said, not in the midst of a church-going population. It may, of course, be suggested, that people go not because of, but in spite of, the great license of manner and freedom of speech in which the Doctor indulges. A commonplace of this kind is scarcely worth refuting. Those who use it can, if they are open to conviction, be convinced that they are in error by the reasonable act of going to the Temple and observing for themselves. I have been there several times, and have come to the conclusion that it is the Parkerisms of the

Doctor which constitute the centripetal force which draws to the Temple from all quarters of London his tens of hundreds. This is written on the faces of the congregation in characters so broad and luminous that the reading is easy indeed. Deep answers unto deep at the noise of his water-spouts. The Doctor's smiles kindle every eye; and when he is about to make a point, the touch of Ithuriel's spear is felt before it pricks. His laugh does not startle as though it were a desecration of the sanctuary, but awakens an echo in every pew and shakes the sides of the Temple. Were the Doctor shorn of his locks he would lose his strength and be as other men.

The question of spiritual success may undoubtedly be raised. Large and interested congregations may be weighed in the balances of the sanctuary and be found wanting, whatever they may go for in the City Temple. But who is to hold the scales? I do not pretend to do so. It is beyond my ability to pronounce upon the subtleties of spiritual influence. The wind bloweth how it listeth. I cannot venture to say that it does not blow through the lusty trumpet of Dr. Parker.

THE COLONIST AT HOME.

I.

On a certain day I went to the Crystal Palace and was present during several hours of the Foresters' Great Day. It certainly is not my intention to describe the glories of the fête. Señor Romah, the Mexican Athlete of the Golden Wing, I did not so much as see. His marvellous performance on the high bars, although with organ accompaniment, had no attractions for one who has seen African and Asiatic monkeys in their native wilds capering to their own chatter. The grand procession, with full regalia, passed unheeded. What does a colonist, who has cleared whole forests to the tune of the ringing axe, care for a set of silly fellows in green cotton velvet, feathers, and preposterous boots, who never saw a deer outside a cage, lost themselves in a wood, or chased a 'possum up a gum tree. The great comic concert I know nothing about, nor do I wish to know. I can imagine that Mr. Macdermott in "The Jilted Drayman" was dismally funny; but imagination is enough. In my opinion it is the British comic singer who drives men to drink. The Mountaineers of the Apennines probably played "their novel instrument the Ocarine" on the top of the tower. At all events the Ocarine I did not hear. Of the pantomime I had a momentary glance. In that moment a ridiculous policeman was trying to eat a monster pie amidst a shower of blows from a mop. The British pantomime is remarkable for its barrenness. It seldom exceeds the inevitable Bobby, and its freshest joke is still and ever, "I'll run you in!" A colonist, accustomed to revere the law in its executive arm, considers this mocking of the Peeler to be a bad sign for England, and he is never more inclined to play the part of the New Zealander on a ragged arch of London Bridge, than when he already sees the debasement of England in the popular disregard for the policeman. The grand display of all the great fountains I saw, but a colonist has gazed upon Niagara and watched a whale spout in his own seas; consequently, he has no eye for waterworks. Professor Beckwith and family probably appeared in their graceful acts of natation, undressed on the water, saved life from drowning, and swam with hands and feet tied; but I did not constitute myself an eye-witness, and I left the scene of enchantment before the assault of arms began. I wish it to be understood that as a colonist I pour contempt upon all these childish and frivolous amusements. A colonist is a man to whom recreation is unnecessary. He has learnt, in prairies, primæval forests, sheep-walks, unsurveyed lands, and new townships, to support life by communion with outer nature and the inner self.

In going to the Foresters' Great Day, I went to see the English people of the particular class likely to be present at that festival. The way they amused themselves, not the amusements provided for them, was what I wanted to observe. It was also an object of personal interest to note their looks, their manners, their speech, and their temper. There were sixty thousand people present, so my chances were excellent. I wish some one with accurate knowledge would tell me to what particular class the sixty thousand belonged. The Foresters, in their velvet and ostrich-feathers, were no doubt aristocrats—noble fellows worthy of their decorations. Leaving them out, who were the others? I may make one or two further recognitions and exceptions. For instance, I needed no guide to assure me that half a dozen swarthy men and women always by themselves were gipsies—the first I have seen for thirty years, saving their brothers and sisters in India. The chief of the gang was in his best vest with coat-sleeves attached, and had the usual black eyes and white teeth of his race, while the women, although the sun was hot, wore the coarse woollen shawl of broad plaid which they used to wear, as I believe, before the Flood. I met them several times, and their only amusement seemed to be a betting trick as to whether the chief, in black eyes and white teeth, could or could not throw a piece of cork into neighbouring chignons without detection. "Two to one," said he, "I do," and he did it. The gipsies, I was able to fix at once. Soldiers, also, were no mystery—they were not Londoners of any class. One jet-black, wholly-headed, large-heeled individual stood confessed—a negro. Two Orientals, one as big as the Claimant, were conspicuously themselves, as they waddled about in distended tunics and wide other garments, looking not unlike balloons incarnate. An occasional Frenchman crossed my path, scornful, critical, full of cultured contempt for the barbarians, their beer, and their beef. These I knew, as also a scanty sprinkling of season ticket holders who had come with their books and their crochet and found the deluge. But to what particular section of what particular class did the bulk of the sixty thousand belong? To the eye of a colonist, more than a quarter of a century out of England, the majority of the men present were very unlike the Englishmen of the last generation. The younger men were all short and small, sallow-faced, dark-eyed, low-browed,—a puny race of no height or breadth, yet having a certain sharp and wiry look about them. The women were not so stunted and narrowed. Many of them were taller than the men, and most of the rest were as tall as their partners. It was this superiority, probably, which made the youngsters lean upon their sweethearts' arms in the promenade. But the complexions of the women were muddy, and their teeth—alas, what had become of them, or what had happened to them? The day was one for excessive merriment, and consequently every mouth was wide open with laughter, with a result which alarmed me for the stamina of the British race of the class represented—a very large class evidently. The rapid increase of dentists in modern times had its explanation on that day in the Crystal

Palace. I regret to say that the multitude of women showed but few fresh, pretty faces of the old style. Time was when beauty was not the monopoly of any class in England. But these big towns, with their buried streets and huddled homes, their smoke and gas instead of fresh air, and their close-crowded life, are changing all that. London is a monster which is devouring beauty day by day. Should this huge city still persist in growing, the next generation of Londoners—the Londoners who cannot get away from its evils—will be a race of pigmies. I suppose the same sort of damaging effect is taking place in Glasgow, Manchester, Sheffield, Birmingham, Liverpool, and all the overgrown towns. The thing will correct itself in time. These monstrous towns will shortly smother the race. Men will die in them like frogs in the exhausted receiver of an air-pump.

Of the temper of the sixty thousand, up to seven o'clock, a poem might be written. It was simply perfect. Not only was there no fighting, but there was no wrath. Once I heard a wife express herself critically about her husband's conduct, and the husband received the rebuke with the meekness of a lamb. That was the only discord of the day. Nor was this sweetness to be attributed to the absence of beer. The means of hard drinking were everywhere at hand, and there certainly was no cold neglect of the means. The sixty thousand drank, but up to seven o'clock very few were apparently the worse for liquor. One old gentleman had drunk himself into a belief that flies were grouse, and that he was making a big bag with the help of a walking-stick. Another old gentleman, having found it warm, had left his coat and hat in charge of the megatherium, and was to be met wandering in unbuttoned vest amongst the trees. Several were silly; but all were genial and bent on amusement, and surely no crowd was ever more content on fare so simple. The most popular recreation was "Kiss in the ring." I have seen this game in the colonies; but I never saw it carried on with so much enthusiasm as at the Foresters' Great Day. Rings were everywhere; and everywhere there was a perfect devotion to the pleasures of free selection, the chase, the capture, the triumphal return, and the loud-sounding reward. Next in order of popularity was the dance, which was almost a solemnity, so painfully serious were the faces which looked over the shoulders. Concertinas abounded, and wherever there was the veriest mimicry of music there were tripping feet. In fact, without music, a couple walking on the yellow and gritty path would suddenly break into a jig, cut a few capers, and walk on light of heart as of heels. Two or three old grandams, past seventy, renewed their youth for the passing hour, and showed the youngsters what dancing used to be when people really danced and did not bob and wriggle. Third in order of popularity was the skipping-rope. It is the fact that hundreds, possibly thousands, of adults paid a penny for the pleasures of a rapid jump while the long rope was being turned by a couple of men who traded in the amusement. Obviously, what these people from the depths of the big, gloomy town wanted was violent exercise in the free air and sunlight. Motion, circulation of the blood, play of muscle and lung, draughts of atmosphere with some ozone in it, these were the things they craved for as by instinct. It was this hunger and thirst for physical activity which also sent them toiling up the tall tower, labouring at the lumbering four-wheeled velocipedes, and skating on the level floor with the help of a pair of bed truckles fastened to their boots. The holiday, after all, was a struggle to get, in a few hours snatched from a closely packed life, at the true conditions of a healthy physical existence. The sight seemed gay; but its suggestions were gloomy. To see a starving man eat is not an altogether agreeable spectacle, because the fierce satisfaction tells of the gnawing hunger which occasioned the ravenous appetite. A London great day, for the class in the Palace on that day is a humiliating confession of the imperfection of civilization and the things which boasted progress does not change for the better. A colonist has the help of contrast in estimating the value of that national growth of which great cities form so large a part. The heaping of men and women together in great masses in old crowded countries is an obvious evil to a man who has been accustomed to the open spaces of almost unpeopled continents, and the vast size of, it may be, a South African boor, out of each of whose mighty limbs, for which nature has given room, half a dozen of that day's sixty thousand might easily be carved. I am more than ever convinced, since the Forester's Fête, that the time is fast coming when England must be half emptied into the colonies, or lose its old reputation for rearing men.

II.

A STRANGER in this vast London is as much interested in its small as in its great things. To him a crossing-sweeper is a curiosity no less than a prince, and Titiens, the star of the opera, is no more a novelty than an organ-grinder. He looks forward with enthusiasm to the Handel Festival, and he listens with emotion to a German band. As a matter of course he goes to the Exhibition of the Royal Academy and, along with a Royal Duke, he is struck with admiration at the fidelity of Miss Thomson's brush; but for all his devotion to high art he can make one of a crowd of starers at the last photograph in a shop-window. He gapes at the marvels of the General Post Office and opens his eyes in mild wonder at a letter pillar. The Criterion, where Spiers and Pond have built a palace for chops, astonishes him, but he has an eye also for the man with a cook-shop on wheels who boils potatoes. The eloquence of the Commons he listens to with mingled feelings, and his ear is tickled while the illegal huckster at the corner praises his suspected wares. So also with respect to the thundering preacher whose pulpit is a flower-pot and whose church is a temple, and the Sunday itinerant who takes his stand on a stool and whose pews are on the pavement,—the Colonist at Home heeds them both. The little and the great together make his sight-seeing and his ear-hearing. And colonists abroad like to be told that the London they cannot see is not all grandeur and greatness. Accordingly I may venture to say that one Sunday I patiently stood out four open-air lectures from as many teetotalers. I was on my way to hear a member of Parliament, who is also a Queen's Counsel, preach in a strikingly pretty new church, when I was arrested by the gesticulations of an orator in a straw hat, around whom had gathered a crowd of hearers. The temptation to do a little vagabondizing was too much for a poor colonist accustomed to outdoor ways, and I took up my place on a neighbouring curb-stone.

The orator in the straw hat was, I found, the conductor of a band of brothers, and was evidently a mechanic. All the orators were mechanics. To my mind they seemed honest men, doing what they did from a sense of duty with a smack of pleasure. Their pulpit was one of the rudest things in carpentry,—a brown old form with a slight rail. To the cross piece in front was attached a bill announcing a forthcoming excursion to some seaside place. On the form there was a bundle of magazines ready for distribution. While the conductor was at work, one of the company circulated a fly-leaf having on one side an advertisement of " the largest and most comprehensive temperance newspaper —the *Templar*," and on the other side a list of answers to the question, " What do the great doctors say?" Unfortunately, every decent thing men can do is abused. A theatre tout had followed the conductor and his band, and as I came up he was busy thrusting into everybody's hand a playbill of the Britannia, announcing " Othello," an opera bouffe, and " The Mountain Robber." The conductor, on seeing this, repudiated the transaction in a manner and temper creditable to him. Upon this the tout slunk off.

Let me say that, although the virtue of teetotalism was their text, two of the orators at all events did not confine themselves to the merely secular side of the question. Their addresses were teetotal speeches with a dash of piety, something like what Dr. Arnold wanted in literature—books with religion in them. The most vigorous of their denunciations were hurled at the publican. The drunkard had their pity and good wishes; but for the drink-seller with his palace, his gaudy wife, his bedizened and bewitching barmaid, his fiery compounds, his hypocritical jollity, and his gross selfishness, the orators had nothing but scorn and indignation. Beer and gin were analysed, exposed, and shown to be foul adulterations. But the publican was worse than the sourest beer or the most vitriolic gin. He was a thing for loathing and curses. He was the man who battened on crime, rottenness, and death.

I could see very well that, while these hot words were being uttered, there was a good deal of sympathy in the crowd. About a hundred men were present; some were roughs, others were costers; more than twenty were sodden or inflamed with debauch, and these were the men who nodded their soaked heads in sullen assent to the charges against the publican. One of the orators drew a picture of the serpent and its fascinations. All the orators were fond of figures from natural history, and this one revelled in a story of the snake and the bird—the beautiful, flashy, glistening, bright-glancing snake and the poor, foolish, fluttering, feeble bird which fell into the open jaws and upon the poisonous fangs. The serpent was the publican whose fascinations were in his gilded hell, his dashing fittings, the glitter of glass and burnished metal, the glare of gas, his own smirk and smile, and the well-garnished charms of buxom wife and breezy barmaid. Yes, here was the serpent, and the poor fool of a working-man was the silly bird that came and looked, and dropped, and died! "Beware the serpent, my fellow working-man!" said the orator. The publican's Sunday cart, and the publican's Sunday nag, and the publican's Sunday harness came in for their share of opprobrium. What were they all, but the profits reaped from the working-man's ruin? When the money is all gone, "Let the fool rot" is the publican's blessing. There can be no doubt about it, the licensed victualler was well banned on that Sunday morning.

One of the orators was fond of statistics, and told the audience how much more the nation spent on beer, wine, and spirits, than it did on bread, butchers' meat, and groceries. He showed how much a man could save in a day, a week, a year, by putting by his drink money. Another orator was great upon the perfect organization of the teetotaller and his self-control. He had a head, and it didn't ache, and he knew what to do with it. His hands and his legs were his own, and he was their master. The same with his tongue. One of the orators could see through a beer-barrel, and knew what beer was. A man would have to drink eight pints of the best malt liquor before he could get at the nourishment there was in a penny loaf. Some of the crowd seemed to think that they would like their penny loaves that way.

The fourth orator was the best dressed of the company, and he was able to say that he had risen from a coal-pit to respectability on teetotal principles. After all the orators had well spoken, a sudden thought seemed to strike the conductor. "Was not this Hospital Sunday, and were they not making collections in all the churches? Why should not they have their collection for the Teetotal Hospital?" "Good!" said a companion, who was not an orator, and out came from the tail of his coat a regular wooden begging-box. The coin chinked merrily into the bit of deal, everybody seeming glad to give something. The conductor told the audience that every penny should be accounted for and acknowledged in the *Templar* or some other paper. After a few minutes the announcement was made that 17s. 6d. had been collected. This cheered the conductor to begin again. He drew a picture of the misery in Bethnal Green, where the people lived apparently on gin and lucifer matches. He then flowered into mythology, which he believed was "queer history," and told a story of one Midas, who could carry a heifer home, and kill it with a blow of his mighty fist. "And who was Midas, my friends? Why, a water drinker." The conductor's mythology was a little off its legs with respect to names, but Milo or Midas it was no matter—there was the moral of the joke as transparent as water itself. From mythology he passed easily to the "Arabian Nights," and introduced

Sinbad and the old man who would stick on poor Sinbad's shoulders. "Who is your old man, my fellow-worker?— why, the publican." It always came round to the publican, and the orator, who came round to him oftenest and gave him the soundest punishment, was an ex-public-house fitter. He knew all the ways of the fellow and his barmaid, and knew all about the fittings. His trade had revealed secrets, and he was not at all unwilling to let some of them out. He had left the rascally business of helping to make gin-palaces look beautiful, and he was doing ten times better than ever he had done in his life.

After listening and learning for an hour I left, and as I did so the box was going round for a second time, very much, I hope, to the advantage of the Teetotal Hospital. There was nothing in the appearance or conduct of the band to lead me to suspect their motives.

AT LOOE WITH THE PILCHARDS.

Where is Looe? and what are pilchards? are questions which would puzzle some modern members of Parliament. In the good old days of rotten boroughs, however, Looe was known as well as London to those who wished to enter the Commons. Before the Reform Bill, this now obscure little Cornish fishing town returned two members to the House, and thus had more than one voice in the councils of the nation. At present it is known only by its pilchards, and they have but a limited reputation—undeservedly so, for the pilchard is a generous, tasty, and nourishing little fish, notwithstanding its bones, which cannot be denied. It is no part of my work to give lessons in geography; so Looe must be dismissed with the prophecy that in less than ten years it will be a fashionable watering-place, with a railway, bathing machines, hotels, and a German band. But I am in the way of duty in bringing pilchards out of the curing cellars of Looe and recommending them to popular notice. Were it possible to send the world to that or any other Cornish fishing town, the pilchard might be allowed to announce itself. It is a fine, oily fish, and fills the air with its flavour. Probably the pilchard is, in this respect, the most bountiful of its kind. After a minute on the grill, its subtle essences penetrate to wonderful distances.

But my first introduction to the pilchards at Looe was not at the delicious moment when the gridiron was turning them into unctuous delicacies, but under less agreeable circumstances. Strolling along the quay, I came upon a dozen fisherman busily engaged in the work of washing the cured fish in hollow wickerwork baskets and huge tubs of salt water. The pilchards were brought on to the quay from neighbouring cellars in large trays, five or six hundred at a time. The trays were inverted, and the fish thrown out in great heaps, yellow with salt, saturated with their oil. The washers put them into the baskets, and then, dipping them into the great tubs of brine, shook them heartily, tossed them up with vigorous jerks, and, having freed them from the clinging salt, returned them to the trays, which were carried back to the cellars. The work went on briskly, the heaps of fish coming and going in surprising quantities. Some of the washers carried on their business at the river itself, standing in the water knee deep and plying their baskets there. The labour was hard, back-breaking, and unpleasantly damp. After a word or two of curious questioning, the result of which must be told by-and-by, I followed the tray-carriers to the cellars, and asked leave to enter. Cheerful permission was given, and I found myself in the presence of millions of fish piled up in tiers against one side of the cellar, twenty or thirty deep and reaching to the ceiling. The front ranks pointed their sharp noses at me out of the midst of the salt with a comical fierceness. There they had been for thirty days, layer upon layer, with salt between, their oil draining away into appointed channels, and the salt biting into them and making them pungent and sound. The last of the thirty days having come, the wall was being broken down. On the floor lay heaps of the fish in their loosened salt. These the men who carried the trays were sieving in sieves to get rid of as much of the salt as possible. Then the trays were filled, and carried out to the tubs on the river-side for the process already described.

In another part of the cellar, another part of the curing business was going on in the hands of the women. Good-tempered dames they were, with arms large enough for a hero and hands hard and ruddy with brine. To these were brought back the sieved and washed fish, looking fairly clean and bright. The wives took the pilchards five at a time by their tails, opened out their bodies into a fan-like shape, and then placed them in the white, new barrels, about twenty of which stood in a row against the wall. In went the fish five at once, on the floor of the barrel, in beautiful order and compactness—the first making a bed for the others. As each barrel holds about 3000 fish, packing takes time; and so, with a "Thank you" and a "Good day," I quickly finished my first object lesson in pilchard curing. Of course I asked many questions, and obtained answers, the pith of which will be given directly. The answers were most kindly and readily given. Indeed, a familiarity with pilchards must, I should say, be an admirable softener of the manners, for Looe has not a surly person in it.

A day or two after, I ventured into another curing shed, and saw the process of pressing the fish tightly down into the barrels. This was done by powerful leverage. The rich oil flowed out plentifully, and this was caught in channels which sloped towards tubs sunk in the ground. A man was ladling out the oil as I passed into an inner shed, where I found another company of women engaged in packing barrels. Scarcely had I said " Good day " when one of the women seized my boot and wiped it with a cloth. "That is the custom here, sir," said she. "It's always the custom when gentlemen come into the cellars to wipe their boots." "And a very good custom it is," said I. "Oh yes; it's the custom," she replied, insisting upon it that it was no individual act of her own, but solely "the custom." What I gave the honest woman shall only be known when what the good men do can no longer be hid. Having seen more walls of pilchards, and more packing by fives into the barrels, and having paid my tribute to the "custom" of the pilchard cellar, I was satisfied with my second object lesson, and quitted school for the day.

The next time I walked the Looe quay, I was fortunate enough to see what was done with the barrels. A crowd about a ship's side attracted my attention, and on joining I found that my salted, sieved, washed, and tightly packed acquaintances were being shipped for Fowey as their first stage on their way to the Mediterranean. The white, new barrels, a little soiled with oil drainings, were brought down from the cellars by the big, brawny fishermen—four men to each barrel. At the ship's side they were weighed, to see if each contained the regulation quantity. This shipping of its great export seemed to be a sight for Looe, as there were ten lookers-on to one worker. I understood the feeling, as after watching the poor dear fish through all the processes of curing, I had a melancholy pleasure in seeing the last of them, and could easily sympathize with the good men who had caught as well as cured them.

All fish may be said to be at their best when fresh, and pilchards are certainly no exception to the rule. Taken from the boat, with the dew of the sea still upon them, and with no more handling than is necessary to remove the head and viscera, and pop them into the frying-pan, they are savoury to a degree. It is a pity that London has no chance of knowing how toothsome a fried, fresh pilchard is. Opportunity alone is wanted to create a liking. As a rule, however, the really fresh pilchard is well known only in Cornwall and West Devonshire. In the season, a proportion of the fish is distributed amongst the western towns and villages nearest to the fishing places. I cannot discover that any reach the Eastern or Northern markets. The extension of railways to Looe, and other similar seats of the pilchard fishery, will make a difference in this respect.

A common way of preparing and preserving the fish for home use, is that of cleaning and salting them. After they have been beheaded, scooped, and washed, they are lined with salt and placed in "a stain," or large earthenware jar, or wooden keg, a layer of fish alternating with a layer of salt. As the salt dissolves, the fish becomes covered with brine. A good stock of salted pilchards is a grand thing in the Cornish fisherman's house, and can go into store for use at any time. Another method of treating this most accommodating fish is that of "scrawing," by which the pilchard is cleaned, split, sprinkled with salt and pepper, and hung in the sun. A broiled, scrawled pilchard would make the fortune of a restaurant, at a price. At Looe, it is considered to be a charming way of serving up the favourite. But the "*marinated* pilchard" is the surpassing delicacy. The phrase is in common use in Cornwall, and half of it has been borrowed from France. Whether the West-country housewives learned the process from an exiled *chef* or not, I cannot tell; but this I know that only a Cornish or West Devonshire housewife knows how to prepare the dish. It is easy to say that the *marinated* pilchard is one which has been baked in a vinegar punch, in which spices and bay leaves have their appointed place. The result is a keen pleasure for the palate.

There is no reason why this dish should not be enjoyed in other places than the far west. Those who have tasted it long for it, and by hook or crook, barrel or jar, marinated pilchards find their way to enthusiastic west-countrymen in London and elsewhere. Nor must the "fair-maid" be forgotten. There is a particular variety of the prepared pilchard, which rejoices locally in that name. It is, as far as I can make out, smoked, and the exiled *chef* from France has, probably, to be referred to for the process and the name. An attempt, which deserves to be successful, is now being made by Messrs. Fox and Fry, of Mevigissey, to prepare and box the fish as sardines. There is a tradition that pilchards were once eaten with cream, in Cornwall; I am sorry to find that this is a forgotten art. But the most important mode of treating the pilchard is that to which I first of all referred. Pilchard-curing is a Cornish industry, and the exportation of the cured fish is no small part of Cornish trade. The barrels, which have a fifty-gallon capacity, and hold about 3500 fish, weighing 476 lbs., are shipped in large numbers to Mediterranean ports, chiefly Italian, I believe. The average price of a barrel of cured pilchards is about fifty shillings, being at the rate of six fish a penny. Whether London would relish what some parts of Italy like, I cannot say, but it is evident that the nearer market could be supplied at a much smaller addition, for carriage and profit, on the fifty shillings, than it is necessary to charge to the more distant ones. Cured pilchards at three a penny, in London, would yield a handsome profit on the outlay at Looe, Polperro, or Fowey. The price of fresh pilchards at Looe, over the side of the boat, is, just now, about ten or eleven shillings the thousand, or about eight a penny. It may be as well to say that a moderate-sized pilchard is about the size of a small herring. Of course, price depends on supply, and of late the finds have not been so plentiful as they once were. But from July to January, and later, the boats go out three or four times every week from all the Cornish ports, and seldom return without a haul. Looe has eighteen or twenty "drivers"—as the boats are called—in full work. Fine boats they are, fit for any weather and any sea, and each one has a crew of four sturdy fishermen. Now, Looe is but one of a score of fishing ports, and is by no means the most important. The fishing-ground is limited to the Cornish and West Devonshire coast, but it is not to be supposed that it is narrow and easily exhausted. The pilchard is a most prolific fish, and could supply an English demand without withdrawing itself from Mediterranean markets. Possibly, these few notes on a neglected British fish may suggest to London caterers the way to a new source of profit. I may just add that the largest number of pilchards captured at any time by one boat, is 80,000. This appears to have been a gigantic exception, and it reads like a miracle. Another boat is said to have brought back, after a night with the net, no less than 40,000. Smaller figures satisfy the fishermen of Looe.

SOUTH AFRICAN PROGRESS AND NATIVE MANAGEMENT.

Read before the Royal Colonial Institute.

South Africa is the Cinderella of the British Colonial family. She is generally ignored, unappreciated, or scolded by her big and ugly relatives. Without strain, the comparison may be continued. Cinderella in due time eclipsed her sisters by the brilliancy of her fortune. She it was who charmed and married the Prince. So also is it reserved for South Africa to become the most splendid of all colonies. Those who hear these words are laughing in their sleeves at least; just as the jealous sisters laughed at the very notion of Cinderella's foot fitting the glass slipper. But however obscure Colonial South Africa may be at the moment, it is destined to grow until it becomes the dominant power in all Africa, facing Europe over the Mediterranean and Asia over the Red Sea. When that day comes, several Princes will be anxious to marry her who is now but a little kitchen wench among the cinders.

The reason for this belief is founded on the unconquerable vitality of the particular European elements in the settlements of South Africa, especially upon the facts to which that vital force has already given birth. The little leaven will leaven the whole lump. This is no theory. The process is going on and will go on. It would not be reasonable to be so confident were South Africa held like an Indian presidency by military force. It is possessed, occupied, settled, turned into a dwelling-place, a home, a country; and its European communities are not regiments or services, but complete societies planted and rooted in the soil, multiplying and spreading with the vigour of a richly endowed nature, easily mastering the other forces with which it comes in contact.

Without the evidence of facts these assertions would be mere bombast. Let us, then, rapidly glance at what South Africa has already become,—what has been accomplished, acquired by it, and what influence it has obtained over its native peoples. And here let it be said that it would be vain indeed to talk of European colonization spreading and establishing itself throughout Africa, unless there was reason to be confident that mere conquest and territorial possession can be accompanied by the art of breaking in, taming, and training the natives to co-operation. In one very important respect Africa is unlike America and Australia. It is inhabited by peoples who are to be counted by the million, and who are not accommodating enough to perish as the white man flourishes. The development of colonization and the progress of dominion must include the wise management of the natives for their good. Had South Africa no proof to show of its ability for this work, its best friends might well be silent about its future. Happily, however, it has such proof. It has not only added territory to territory and pushed its frontier lustily to the North, but it has also, by an honest purpose, firm endeavour, and fair skill, given newness of life to large bodies of African natives.

In the first place, however, let me direct attention to the size and expansiveness of the South African settlements,—to the advancing tide of European occupation, as also to the signs of that growing wealth, power, and enterprise, which promise to give to that tide a perpetual flow.

The coast line of British South Africa curving from the mouth of the Orange, which opens into the Atlantic, to that of the Tugela, which empties itself into the Indian Ocean, is not much less than 2000 miles in length. It must not be supposed, however, that British South Africa is merely a littoral strip, with here and there, at distant intervals, a coast trading station. From the southernmost point where Cape Agulhas fronts the Southern Ocean, the Cape and Natal traverse the interior over a distance of quite 500 miles, while the inland frontier chord, from foot to foot of the great arc, is 1000 miles long. Within this sea coast and landward boundary of 3000 miles there are quite 300,000 square miles of absolutely British territory. British South Africa—which is not the whole of Colonial South Africa—is therefore a vast possession and a splendid starting-point for civilization.

In this large land her Majesty has more than a million subjects, one-fourth being of European blood. The Cape, Natal, and Griqualand West are dotted over with towns, villages, and homesteads, and are traversed by roads. Colonization has not tarried by the sea-shore, but has its settlements on the remotest points of the inland frontier. Industry has taken set forms everywhere within the boundaries, and commerce with its usual enterprise has pushed its operations far beyond the border. Three railway lines are being constructed and three more are being surveyed, the Cape Colony alone venturing upon an expedition in this department of £5,000,000. The telegraphic wires have a length of 2000 miles. The products and exports of the settlements are various, and some have a certain splendour of attraction. They include wool, wheat, and wine, diamonds, ostrich-feathers, and ivory, copper and gold, coffee and sugar, fruit and fish, cattle, sheep, horses, and ostriches. The total annual value of the British South African exports and imports is no less than fifteen millions sterling. The total annual value of its products used in home consumption is probably an equal sum. The landed, house, and stock property, and public works of the three English colonies, represent an estimated investment of more than 150 millions. The annual revenue of the Cape, Natal, and Griqualand West together is more than a million and a half. There are some States in Europe of historic name which do not enjoy the public income of these obscure British colonies. Greece, Norway, Switzerland, and Saxony are in some cases poorer and in all not richer, in this respect, than the Cape, about which ninety-nine out of every hundred Englishmen know little more than that it is somewhere in Africa, or than that it was once the halfway house to India. Portugal, formerly the mother of colonies, can but boast a revenue of three times that of British South Africa; and Belgium, that hive of industry, and Holland, once the owner of the Cape, can only count five times as many millions. The importance of this revenue fact will be all the more recognized when it is borne in mind that it represents an annual sum contributed by British South Africa entirely from its own resources, and expended entirely on government, the administration of law, the protection of life and property, the promotion of education, the maintenance of postal lines, and the construction of harbours, roads, bridges, railways, and telegraphs. The comparatively large sum is the organized State contribution of the British possessions to the great civilizing institutions and agencies at work in South Africa. And it is steadily increasing. The institutions of British South Africa are liberal and fairly vigorous. The Cape Colony has a constitution similar, in some of its broad features, to that of England. It has a responsible Ministry and a Legislature of two Chambers. The form of Government in Natal is after a narrower type, while that of Griqualand West is still more official. District or county affairs are in the hands of divisional councils, and many of the towns have mayors and corporations. Education boasts one university, several colleges and high schools, and a system of grants in aid which is considered to be admirable. Religious agencies abound, as there is scarcely a denomination in England which is not represented in South Africa. The Anglican Church has there six bishops and the Church of Rome three, while of other bodies, the Wesleyan Church alone has there a hundred clergymen. Of newspapers British South Africa has no less than forty. The commercial institutions include all the customary agencies of trade, banking, and insurance. Corporations well known in London, such as the Standard Bank, the London and South African, and the Oriental, have their branches in almost every town of any size, and the local companies are numerous and thriving. The important interests of communication with England are served by two steam lines, worked by the Union Company and by Donald Currie and Co., and affording weekly arrivals and departures. European immigration is promoted by an annual vote of £25,000 and the maintenance of an efficient agency in London. Here I mark a stage in the argument. I have given a catalogue—a mere list—of some of the facts of effective colonization presented by British South Africa. May I not venture to say that if the great mid-continent is to be subdued to civilization, a foothold has been gained from which a series of steps forward, by-and-by to become "leaps and bounds," may be expected to be made?

Another group of similar facts has yet to be mentioned. To the north of British South Africa are two hardy and vigorous offshoots of colonization—the Orange Free State and the Transvaal Republic, both independent communities, using the Dutch language because chiefly of Dutch descent, but having within and about them powerful English influences. These republics have a white population of singular aptitude for the rough and ready outwork of colonization, and numbering from fifty to sixty thousand. Their joint area is not less than 220,000 square miles. Each State has a settled Government. The President of the Free State was formerly a distinguished pleader at the Cape bar. The President of the Transvaal was formerly a distinguished clergyman of the Cape Dutch Reformed Church. Both are born subjects of her Majesty. The discovery of gold at Marabastad and Leydenburg has given new attractions to a country of wonderful fruitfulness. President Burgers is now on his way to Europe for the purpose of arranging, if possible, for a railway from his capital and the Gold Fields to Delagoa Bay. The most advanced point of the Transvaal Republic is 100 miles north of the tropic of Capricorn and not more than 300 miles from the Victoria Falls on Livingstone's Zambezi; while Zoutspanberg, the at present uppermost township of the Republic, is scarcely 400 miles from the Kongone mouth of that famous river. A distance of 300 or 400 miles in Africa is comparatively small when the rate at which settlement advances is considered. The Limpopo, which now bounds the pioneer State of European South Africa, is about 1000 miles north of Cape Agulhas, and of that 1000 miles more than 500 have been added to European possession and rule within less than 40 years. It will not take another 40 years for the vanguard of colonization to reach the Zambezi River, whose sources are in the very centre and heart of

Africa. At this moment the Limpopo is being crossed by the scouts of occupation. Hunters, traders, and missionaries have their stations beyond it; and, so it is reported, bands of fanatics—a class from which the forerunners of civilization, themselves not always civilized, frequently spring—are, according to their quaint ideas, heading northwards, first for Egypt, then for Jerusalem, camping by the way, and leaving marks of travel and rest which in time will become roads and townships. Possession and political boundaries are always preceded by these irregular skirmishers. The limits of a paper do not admit of much elaboration, but I hope that enough has been said to show that, as the two Republics are the result of the restless, migratory habits of the colonists of the Cape, so also, from the same cause, will they certainly be the sources from which an upward-flowing stream of pioneering life will continue to issue.

I now come to another part of the argument, which is that the South African colonies have before them a great work in the whole continent because they show, not only the ability to acquire territory and accumulate the means of material prosperity and self-culture, but also an aptitude for the management of the natives.

It is but little understood in England that of all parts of the empire, India and Ceylon excepted, South Africa contains the largest number of natives under British rule. The North American Indians in the Dominion of Canada, the Coolies of Mauritius, the Maories of New Zealand, the savages of Australia, the negroes of the West Coast Settlements of Africa are, respectively, not to be compared, as far as number goes, to the native peoples of British South Africa. Counting together the forces of the various tribes and remnants of tribes, there are in the Cape Colony, Natal and Griqualand West, quite a million of natives subject to the Queen's Government, while nearly another million in the neighbouring territories of Kaffirland Proper and Zululand may be said to be more or less amenable to British authority and influence. Not only as to number, but in respect to everything which makes the subjection of native races interesting and important, the Cape and Natal present large facts. That is to say, the natives in those colonies are not merely there, but they are there as the objects of government and social experiment. They are thought about, acted upon, made the subjects of systems, schemes, and institutions. In the Cape Administration there is a Native Department, and there is a Native Department in the Natal Administration. It is acknowledged in both colonies that the presence of a million barbarians necessitates the creation of an especially adapted agency in the State, and that any attempt to deal with these people as if they were on a similar footing with the colonists, on the ground of a common humanity, would be a ruinous piece of *doctrinaire* affectation or fanaticism. The manhood of the African native is never for a moment ignored by any party, political arrangement, judicial institute, or social custom of the colonies. But it is clearly seen that he is an African native and not a man of European heritage, in blood and training. Accordingly he has a department in the Government all to himself. There is not only a Secretary for Native Affairs in the Cape Ministry, but there are Commissioners, Governor's Agents, Magistrates, Residents with chiefs, charged to administer justice and maintain order among native communities, according to an unwritten law in which native precedents and customs are regarded so far as they are right in principle. There are schools for the natives. There are missionaries to the natives. There are native taxes. There are lands reserved for the natives. There is a method of converting natives into citizens. And yet it would not be true to say that the institutions and agencies of either the Cape or Natal are, in themselves or in the spirit in which they have been fashioned, intentionally separative. The object of all alike, whether Government officers or missionaries, political institutions as well as religious, is indeed to make the African as much like the European as possible. The purpose of the special departmental agency is to work out all causes of difference in the State. The people of England need not be alarmed when they are told that in the South African colonies there is a class of her Majesty's subjects under exceptional treatment. There is especial care, but no oppression; guardianship, but no denial of right. Now and then ordinary processes and conditions are disturbed; the barbarian makes a mistake and the colonist blunders. Then comes a period of confusion and apparent wrong. Force takes the place of kindly law and system. The whole scene of disorder is aggravated by the rude conditions of colonial life. English sentiment is startled into more or less vehement indignation.

Probably it is well that England should be sensitive. But it should be remembered that even in modern times England has had her seasons of great social and political disturbance, in which floundering and blundering, passion and force, have had their day. It is right for England to preserve for herself and for her colonies a high standard of opinion with respect to justice, equality, and liberty. Only let England temper her judgments of others with the lessons of her own history.

Allowances being made for average exceptions, British rule in South Africa is entitled to be called beneficent. It is, in many important respects, worthy to be classed with British rule in India, of which England may well be proud. As brilliant it is not and cannot be at present. But when the obvious differences are put on one side, there stands out, to those who know what is being done in both lands, the happy fact that scarcely a single effort is put forth by Government or any institution of society which is not intentionally directed to the elevation and betterment of the natives. The principles and aims of the Government of India are well known in England. The same cannot be said of the character and purposes of the British Government in South Africa. The general English ignorance of the fact that her Majesty has a million native subjects in the Cape and Natal is necessarily accompanied by an almost utter ignorance as to the manner in which the responsibilities of government are met.

The Cape Government has not only a Native Department briskly at work, but it publishes a Blue-Book on

Native Affairs. I do not hesitate to say that this official annual has in it information which can claim to be as interesting and as important to British readers as half the material which continental correspondents contribute to the *Times*, the *Daily News*, the *Standard*, and the *Telegraph*. The way in which colonial Englishmen are governing hundreds of thousands of Africans ought to be of as much moment to Englishmen at home as the intrigues of French parties or the fights of Spanish factions. The affairs of Europe must needs be represented in English papers, but space might very well be found for the vigorous efforts of British colonists to add to territorial conquests the better triumphs of civilization over the tribes they have subjugated. In the Blue-Book published last year there is a remarkable account of the advance made by good government in British Fingoland over the Kei, and in Basutoland over the Orange. Every word is worth reading by every Englishman. The story of the Fingo settlements is indeed a brilliant page in the annals of the Cape. The Fingoes were, in the terrible times of Matuana and Chaka, driven southward from Zululand into the territory of the Galeikas, a Kaffir tribe close upon the borders of the Cape. Received as outcasts, they were made slaves and called "dogs," which is the proper meaning of the word "Fingoes." The treatment awarded to them was worse than that given to dogs. Life became intolerable to them, and in their misery they appealed to the neighbouring colony. This was in 1834. The British Government interfered on their behalf, and the result was that the Galeikas fell upon the unfortunate people and murdered them by tens and scores. Expostulation was answered by the Chief Hintza with the insolent reply, "Well, and what then—are they not my dogs?" Sir Benjamin d'Urban, the then Governor, seized this chief and kept him and his son and 150 of their people as hostages, and let it be known that he intended to shoot any two of them for every Fingoe killed after three hours' notice. (Sir Benjamin d'Urban was the man for his place, and as a matter of course he was called and disgraced. This by the way.) His vigorous threats were successful. The massacre of the Fingoes was stopped. The next step with Sir Benjamin was to deliver "the dogs" from their masters. The Fingoes, led by the missionary Ayliff, whom a not ungrateful people to this day called their Moses and Aaron, marched out of Kaffirland into the colony—they, their women and their children, as poor a crowd as ever fled from bondage. The Cape Colony gave them shelter, protection, land, employment, education, religion, citizenship, and free manhood. I must press the events of years into a few words. The fugitives from Chaka and the dogs of Hintza became men from the day when they crossed the Kei. But this is not all. In time the lands of Peddie, Newtondale, and Kamastone became too narrow for the Fingoes. British rule preserved them and gave them liberty to increase and multiply. There was no room for them, their herds and their flocks, and they wanted more lands for their picks and ploughs. Then—about ten years ago—there was another Fingo march. The Colonial Government moved some thousand of them into a fruitful and pleasant district over the Kei, settled them under British magistrates, encouraged them to industry and the acquisition of property, and helped them to that start which is at once the difficulty and secret of progress. The measure has been most successful. Under the guidance of wise officers—which is the first and last of the Cape native system—the Fingoes of the Transkei have become a prosperous people, using ploughs, shearing wool, buying and selling, building houses, furnishing them, making roads, paying taxes, supporting schools, and attending churches. I do not mean to say that Fingoland is a Paradise. It is a very long way from being so. But it may confidently be claimed as a witness to the ability of the Cape to deal with the native question in practice.

I turn now to Basutoland. Some years ago the Basutos were reduced to starvation by a long war with the Free State. The Cape Government stepped in and by the charm of annexation rescued the remnants of a once flourishing tribe from destruction. A part of their country fell into the hands of the conquering Boers. Over what was left the British flag was hoisted. The next step was to appoint prudent British men—commissioners and magistrates—to take the starving, unhoused, and fever-stricken people in hand. This was seven years ago, and what now? What has been the result of placing these people, not theoretically, but actually, under the care of wise English colonists? The Blue-Book shall give the answer. Mr. Griffith, the Governor's agent in Basutoland, says:—"At the present moment a thorough confidence in the Government and its administration of the laws seems to prevail everywhere. As a mark of this, I may adduce that the paramount chief, Letsie, was without difficulty induced to apprehend his own nephew, a young chief named Sekake, who was charged with the crime of murder, but was subsequently convicted of culpable homicide, and sentenced to two years' imprisonment with hard labour. The revenue is collected without difficulty; crime, especially stock-stealing, is rare; and both chiefs and people submit gladly to the laws. From returns which have been sent in to me by the different magistrates, I find that during the year only five cases of stealing were reported from the Free State, and in most of these cases the stolen property was recovered before the thefts were reported by the owners. When it is considered that the boundary line common to the Free State and Basutoland extends from the Orange River to the sources of the Caledon, a distance of at least 180 miles, it must be admitted that the Basutos have no longer any right to be called 'a nation of thieves,' which was the title given them by the Free State a few years ago. Materially as well as politically there has been progress. Where only half a dozen small shops once existed, some fifty respectable trading stations have now sprung up, the buildings erected at which give a different aspect to the country. Hundreds of waggons enter Basutoland, and traverse it in every direction, collecting and exporting the grain of the country to the Free State and the Diamond Fields. The production of grain is greatly increased, the plough having generally superseded the Kaffir pick. Flocks and herds, which had disappeared from the country during the war, now dot the face of the landscape in every direction. Stone cottages are beginning to supplant the rude native 'hut,' and the Basutos present the general appearance of a thriving and well-ordered people. The discovery of the Diamond Fields has had a great effect upon the country; money has come into general use, and commerce has been much facilitated and increased thereby. The trade of this territory, one of the principal granaries of the Diamond Fields, has been very largely developed during the past year. In 1872 there were thirty fixed trading stations in the country, a number which, during the past year, has increased to fifty. Merchandise to the value of about £150,000 has been imported into the country during the same period. The exports have been about 2000 bales of wool, and upwards of 100,000 muids of grain (wheat, mealies, and Kaffir corn), also a considerable number of cattle and horses. The articles which the Basutos obtain from the traders are almost entirely either of British or foreign manufacture, and consequently the colonial revenue must benefit very considerably by the Basuto trade. The revenue collected in 1873 has exceeded that collected in 1872 by £2953. Larger arrears of land are brought under cultivation each year, and consequently the demand for ploughs continues unabated, and the production of grain is annually increasing. Last year the number of ploughs purchased by the Basutos from the traders in Basutoland was 600; this has been carefully ascertained from actual returns furnished by the traders themselves."

With reference to education the report has much to say, but I can find room for only a very few sentences. "Besides the general process of instruction carried on in primary and infant schools at all the stations and outstations in the country, and which are regularly attended by nearly 2000 children, there are," says Mr. Griffith, "also two important training institutions, established at Morija and Thaba Bosigo, one for boys and the other for girls, which occupy the best attention of some of the most able and experienced of the missionaries."

So much for the testimony of Basutoland and the Cape Native Blue-Book to the genius of the colony for native management. I shall add nothing to this testimony except to say that the point of its meaning is that a good native system is the setting up of the judgment seat of a man of wisdom and a right spirit. It is not theoretical or institutional elaboration, it is the simplicity and directness of personal influence, backed—and I should like this to be well observed—backed by the presence of power. The Cape Colony is strong in the estimation of Fingoes, Kaffirs, and Basutos, and this conviction, deeply seated in the mind of Fingoland and Basutoland, is of the greatest assistance to the agents and magistrates.

Recent events very naturally suggest the question— What about native rule in Natal? How does that show an aptitude for the work of a civilizing subjugation? This question is a natural one in England, because in England at this time native rule in Natal is supposed to be summed up in the one word "Langalibalele." Very few in this country know what the true history of the natives in Natal has been since 1845, when it was proclaimed a British colony. Thanks to a Bishop's Blue-Book and the enterprising London Press, everybody knows, or thinks he knows, that Natal is a place where gross blunders and worse than blunders are committed under the name of native management—that Natal is the place where chiefs and tribes are desolated by rash governors and panic-stricken colonists. Now, the merits of the Langalibalele affair it certainly is not my intention to discuss. I will only ask for my brother colonists in a much perplexed and greatly tried land a little forbearance from Englishmen who are not colonists. Again and again when I have read the indignant and passionate criticisms of Natal mistakes in the dailies of this city, I have been reminded of an old sea-song which says :—

> "Ye gentlemen of England who live at home at ease,
> How little do you know of the dangers of the seas,
> Where the stormy winds do blow."

Let it be supposed that Natal fell into an error when it dealt with Langalibalele and his people in the way it did. Still the error of 1873 is not the whole of native management in that colony, any more than the mutiny of 1857 is the sum total of British rule in India. The history of Natal in its relations to the natives is in truth singular; and in its general character and broad facts, I claim it as an additional proof of the genius of the British South African colonies for native management.

The native question of Natal cannot be understood

without some knowledge of its geographical position and its surroundings. It is a country of 25,000 square miles, diamond shaped. Of its four sides, one faces the Indian Ocean, and one the Drakensberg Mountains which divide it from the Free State; on the north-east side is Zululand, with its warlike hordes, and on the south-west is savage and independent Kaffirland, full of restless tribes. There is no British colony in the world with surroundings of a more dangerous character.

It must be further and especially observed that Natal is nearly 200 miles from the nearest of the Cape towns, and that the communication between the two colonies is by sea. Natal is thus a comparatively small dependency imbedded in a part of savage Africa. Now then, let us glance at its white population. Thirty years ago it was annexed. At that time the Europeans were not more in number than we are this evening in this room. To-day they are not more than 18,000, all told, men and women, old and young. The Government has been that of a Crown colony, with a difference or two. The salary of the governor was until lately much less than £2,000. It is now not more. The Imperial Government has kept there the wing of a regiment. Well, not to weary you with details, what has this little colony, thus surrounded by dangerous tribes, thus distant from its nearest neighbour, with its handful of whites that would not fill a third-rate town in Dorsetshire, with its underpaid Government and its mockery of a garrison— what, I ask, has it done in the matter of the natives? It has thrown open its passes and river drifts to the hundreds and thousands of refugees who have fled to it from Zulu cruelty and oppression. It has awarded to these people ample locations, thrown over them the shield of the British name, and given protection, quiet, and the means of a rude plenty. To-day there are more than 300,000 natives in Natal, scarcely one of whom has any other right to be there than that allowed him by British clemency. Natal has become a great native preserve, and for thirty years, with but one exception, the colony has kept the peace. With half a million of warlike natives on one side, with a quarter of a million of warlike natives on another side, and with 300,000 savages within it, it has had no war and no civil war, until this misfortune of yesterday. The officer who has been in charge of the Natal Native Department is Mr. Shepstone, a born colonist. He has had no special service to assist him. His own salary has not averaged more than £600 or £700 a year. He has had no police except a few natives. The soldiers of the garrison have not been at his command. Simply by his own sagacity, and with the help of the patience and courage of the colonists, he has afforded shelter to hundreds of thousands of natives, subdued their turbulence, and avoided war with the tribes from which the refugees fled.

Gathering together the evidence which I have thus been able to produce of the ability of the South African colonists not only to possess themselves of territory and to arm themselves with power, but also to yoke in to the work of civilization the aboriginal tribes which neither humanity nor expediency desires to see destroyed, I hope I may venture to reaffirm, with some slight chance of avoiding derision, that Colonial South Africa has before it large relations to the whole of the great African continent.

The few remaining minutes of the hour I may perhaps be permitted to use in referring to one or two measures by which Colonial South Africa might be made more effective for its responsibilities and work.

It must be considered to be a misfortune that there should be a divided rule in South Africa, and that this should give rise to jealousies, misunderstandings, and disputes between the British Colonial Government, the Dutch Republics, and the Portuguese settlements. Such a state of things must be enfeebling and dangerous. Within the last seven or eight years, the causes of quarrel between the Free State, the Transvaal, and the British Government at the Cape have been many and serious, arising chiefly out of boundary questions and native policy. The irritation has occasionally been intense. Should present conditions continue, there will be no security against something much worse than irritation. It is most desirable that now, when the feeling of kinship between all South Africans is strong and warm, the time should be seized for binding together colonies and states in a national union. Even now the difficulties to be overcome are great, but the lapse of time and the inevitable occurrence of fresh quarrels will make them greater. I cannot pretend to know in what way a result much to be wished is to be brought about, but I am assured in my own mind that it would be useless to contemplate anything but kindly, respectful, and conciliatory approaches to the Free State and the Transvaal. Force is out of the question. The Cape Colony and Natal are full of people having close personal and family relationships with the inhabitants of those States, and also strong political and religious sympathies. Besides, to make them effective parts of a national community, they must take their places willingly. The chief obstacle is the flag. The question with each State is the question of abandoning an independent position for a place in a Confederation which would not be independent, but dependent upon England. It is a question of sentiment, and sentiment is a very obstinate as well as a very delicate force. There is no chance for a South African Confederation but through responsible government. The idea of a South African Dominion enjoying the same form of government, the same powers and privileges, as the Dominion of Canada, might, perhaps, if presented to the two Dutch Republics by an accomplished diplomat, skilled in the art of putting things, win from them that hesitation which in some cases is the prelude to consent. The Cape is now practically a self-governing country. The two Dutch States, by becoming like the Cape, and by entering into a federal union with it and with Natal, would lose but little of actual independence, and would be large practical gainers by the alliance. And here I may be permitted to say that I have, since writing this paper, read with great satisfaction the passage in Earl Carnarvon's recent speech in which he said: "Hitherto the interests and systems of all the States in South Africa have conflicted with each other. My wish is to see those interests and systems brought into greater utility. I desire, in the first instance, to see a greater development of those great resources which South Africa possesses. Secondly, I desire to see a uniform system adopted in these States, because as long as different systems exist among them there will be a perpetual source of danger. And, lastly, I must look most earnestly to a better understanding being created between the two Dutch Republics and ourselves. I think it would be to the interests of all parties to concur in demanding that there should be a better understanding and a more conciliatory course of action between those Republics and ourselves." These are judicious and statesmanlike words, and they are backed, if they have not been suggested, by opinions to which Mr. Froude has given an equally earnest and eloquent utterance. Sentiments of this kind from high authority awaken hope.

I confess, however, that I am not sanguine of any near success. Meanwhile, attention and effort might well be directed to the consolidation of the British possessions in South Africa, and chiefly for the sake of efficiency in the important native work in Natal. A few minutes ago I ventured to attribute the marked success of native management at the Cape to personal influence, backed by the presence of power. I said that the Cape was strong in the estimation of Fingoes, Kaffirs, and Basutos, and that this consciousness of strength was important. Now, Natal is not strong in the sense in which the Cape is. The half a million of natives in the Cape are confronted by a quarter of a million of Europeans. The natives of the Cape have been defeated in four great wars. In Natal the 300,000 natives have before them only 18,000 Europeans, and they have not been again and again beaten in the field. Then Natal is separated from the Cape by an intervening, independent, and savage territory of nearly 200 miles in length, except at the point where it touches Basutoland. It is this feebleness and isolation which must be accepted as one of the reasons why Natal has not any such facts to present as those which shine forth so conspicuously from Fingoland and Basutoland. It is a marvel that the little colony has done so much and so well. In order that she should do better, it is necessary to give to her the moral force of a close association with the older, wealthier, and stronger colony. This can only be done by a gradual and speedy incorporation of Kaffirland, from the Kei to the Umtafuna, with the Cape on one side and Natal on the other. This is a process which happily is going on. The Fingo settlement, the Idutchwa reserve, and Griqualand East are virtually British. The Residents with the Tambookie, Galeika, and other Kaffir chiefs, are the agents of British political power, and traders, missionaries, and squatters represent other annexing influences. What should be added to all this is the settled intention to take advantage of every opportunity to complete the work, so that the Cape and Natal may touch each other and form together a compact power. The consolidation of the British possessions would make them irresistible. The Zulus of Natal would understand the change at once. It would act as a charm.

Consolidation, however, cannot be brought about to-day or to-morrow, while the difficulties of native management in Natal are immediate and pressing, as Sir Garnet Wolseley is now discovering. It will be a fortunate thing should he, seeing that he cannot bring the Cape to Natal, be able to introduce into Natal the Cape native system in its thorough efficiency. At the Cape there is in reality a considerable native service, including such men as Brownlee, Griffith, Blyth, Ayliff, Bright, Levey, and a score of others. From this service men of experience are told off to locations where they are devoted entirely to the work of native management and improvement. These officers are animated by an ambition to do their duty. They are not overwhelmed with other employment. In Natal the whole responsibilities of the Native Department fall upon the shoulders of a man who is a member of the general government, and a few men who are magistrates over the Europeans in the district in which they reside. Properly speaking, there is no Native Service in Natal, and it would be unreasonable to expect that a colony of 18,000 whites should be able to support an agency equal to the effective management of a savage population of more than 300,000. Instead of sending marines to the assistance of Sir Garnet, it would be much more to the purpose were the Imperial Government to supply him with the means of establishing a service in the colony entirely devoted to the labours of breaking in, or alluring, the natives to industry, obedience, and decency. The tribal system, and the power of chiefs and headmen, might then be replaced by fair terms of citizenship, and by the influence of men of vigour, conscience, and sagacity. A dozen such men placed about amongst the 300,000 would work a miracle. The Zulus of Natal are closely related to the Fingoes of the Cape, and Mr. Shepstone awaits only the means and the men to repeat in Natal the singular success which Captain Blyth and his coadjutors have commanded in Fingoland. Natal is a Crown colony, and England might well spend for a few years an annual £20,000 on a work for which, after all, she is responsible, and for which she makes herself responsible by occasional interference of a character the most serious.

In concluding these remarks, I may be allowed to say that they take it for granted that the Imperial power will encourage that tendency to expansion which the history of Colonial South Africa exhibits. There was a time, and that not very remote, when England seemed at least to sound a halt. A voice appeared to come from high places saying to "the red line" which marks on all maps the widening boundaries of the Empire,—"Thus far shalt thou go and no further." It is to be hoped that that time has gone by, and that once more it is understood that all British colonies, dependencies, and dominions have full liberty to advance, and rejoice in the pleasures of growth. There is a pleasure in the act of growing. It was my lot to be in India in the time of that great annexationist, the Earl of Dalhousie, and although subsequent events have clouded the splendour of his rule, yet it was splendid, and history in its long run will show it to have been wise as well as brilliant. At all events, no Englishman then on the soil of India could avoid a sense of satisfaction as the Punjaub, Nagpore, Burmah, Pegue, and Oudh were added to the Empire. It has also been my lot to be in South Africa while the Transkei, Basutoland, and Griqualand have been brought under British rule. I have witnessed the hoisting for the very first time of the British ensign over lands at the moment proclaimed to be British territory, and have felt an enthusiasm of which I am not ashamed,—not ashamed, because from an experience of nearly thirty years spent in British dependencies and colonies, I am convinced that, in its grand and lasting characteristics and results, British supremacy everywhere means not the mere lust of territory and pride of conquest, but the enthronement of justice, the softening of manners, and the substitution of a living progress for the dead levels or quick descents of oriental or savage custom.

THE END.

www.ingramcontent.com/pod-product-compliance
Lightning Source LLC
Chambersburg PA
CBHW031930230426
43672CB00010B/1874